The Power of Preparation for Surgery

Getting Your Mind and Body Ready for an Operation and Beyond

DR SUNIL KUMAR WITH DR TONI BRUNNING

Contents

What To Expect vii
About Us ix

Section 1: Prehabilitation and Lifestyle Medicine in Practice 1
1. Prehabilitation 5
2. Pillars of Lifestyle Medicine 17
3. Healthy Nutrition 23
4. Mental Wellbeing and Stress Reduction 37
5. Healthy Relationships and Social Connectedness 43
6. Physical Activity 53
7. The Importance of Sleep 61
8. Minimising Harmful Substances 67
9. Self-Care Strategies 75
10. Collaborating with Practitioners 79
11. Sample Program Template and Intermittent Fasting Guide 83

Section 2: Your Journey to Surgery and What to Expect 99
1. Physical Effects of an Operation 101
2. Psychological Effects of an Operation 111
3. Using the Time Before Your Operation 117
4. Weeks Before Your Operation Date 125
5. Day of Your Procedure 141
6. After Your Procedure 147

Summary and Conclusions 155

Appendices 157
Appendix 1: Glossary of Terms 157
Appendix 2: Prehabilitation Considerations for Different Surgeries 163
Appendix 3: Summary Chart of Prehabilitation and Lifestyle Medicine Approaches 167

Appendix 4: Resources and Support for Patients 171

Acknowledgements **173**

Disclaimer

The information contained in this book is intended for educational and informational purposes only. It is not intended as a replacement for personalised medical advice, diagnosis, or treatment. The reader should not use the information within this book for diagnosing or treating a health problem or disease. While the authors of this book are qualified medical practitioners, the information in this book should not be construed as medical advice. The reader should consult their own healthcare professional for advice and treatment about any medical condition. The authors and publisher of this book are not responsible for any loss, damage, or injury caused by the information in this book.

Copyright © 2024 Dr. Sunil Kumar and Dr. Toni Brunning.

What To Expect...

In this book, we use our knowledge and experience as doctors and lifestyle medicine physicians to help you as much as possible to prepare yourself for a surgical procedure. It is for anyone who is currently on a waiting list for surgical treatment (a LOT of people right now) and also really handy for relatives and carers of anyone who is awaiting an operation. Side benefit: the advice in this book will help you to improve your future health and life too.

Section One... has highly useful and easy to apply lifestyle and medicinal advice and interventions that can help you prepare for surgery. Actually, they apply to everyone, so you can benefit even if you are not waiting for a surgical procedure now. The idea is to help you get fit for your surgery and fit for life afterwards!

Section Two... supplies a practical guide that details what to expect around the time of your surgery and explains what is likely to happen during preparation and admission (for surgery), as well as what to expect in your post-operative recovery period.

So let's begin...

About Us

Dr Toni Brunning MBChB FRCA MMEd DipIBLM/ BSLM is a Consultant Anaesthetist at Worcestershire Acute Hospitals NHS Trust, and a trustee and council member of the Royal College of Anaesthetists. She has a Masters in Medical Education and is a Lifestyle Medicine physician, through the International Board of Lifestyle Medicine USA and the British Society of Lifestyle Medicine.

She has an interest in clinician health and well-being and in lifestyle medicine for patients awaiting surgery. She runs national courses that combine education for doctors with promoting the 'pillars of lifestyle medicine' to clinicians. These events empower doctors to take ownership of their own physical and mental health and wellbeing. They provide practical skills and experience as part of their continued professional development. This book shares some of these skills and knowledge with patients to help them prepare their own body and mind for their upcoming surgical procedure and for life beyond.

Toni has personal experience of what it's like on the other side of the table, after she underwent major surgery herself in 2022. Despite being a medical professional who felt she understood the impact of surgery on patients, it gave her greater insight into the patient journey which she shares in this book.

Dr. Sunil Kumar MBBS FCAI FRSA MRCA DipIBLM brings over 20 years of medical expertise to his role as an Associate Specialist Anaesthetist at University Hospitals of Morecambe Bay NHS Trust. As an elected council member of the Royal College of Anaesthetists, he draws on his clinical and leadership experience to help shape anaesthesia policies and practices.

Dr. Kumar's passion extends beyond the operating room into the world of Lifestyle Medicine. As a board certified Lifestyle Medicine physician through the International Board of Lifestyle Medicine USA and the British Society of Lifestyle Medicine, he educates both patients and fellow physicians on leveraging simple lifestyle changes for improved health and wellbeing.

He is a Precision Nutrition trained Health Coach. He utilises his expertise in Lifestyle Medicine as a Lead Tutor for BSLM and Faculty Trainer for the NHS England health and wellbeing workshop series for clinician wellbeing . He also serves as an Advisory Member on Professional Standards for the UK and International Health Coaches Association and an Honorary Ambassador for the Personalised Care Institute.He has authored a The Power of Self-Care : Transforming heart health with Lifestyle Medicine, available internationally with great reviews.

Dr. Kumar empowers people to take control of their health and draws on the latest evidence-based research and his own clinical expertise. As an expert in Lifestyle Medicine and physician well-being, his goal is to inspire readers to embark on their own journey toward better health in preparation for surgery and beyond.

SECTION 1

Prehabilitation and lifestyle medicine in practice

"The good physician treats the disease; the great physician treats the patient who has the disease"

William Osler

When you are waiting for surgery, it is normal to feel a bit helpless. We are here to change that. With the right guidance and information, you can empower yourself to take control of your health, even in the lead-up to your procedure.

We'll be using what we call *prehabilitation,* alongside lifestyle and medicine practices. What this means is that, by focusing on key areas such as healthy nutrition, stress reduction, physical activity, and more, you can make meaningful changes to your lifestyle that not only promote a smoother recovery but can also have lasting benefits on your overall health and wellbeing.

Through this informative and practical guide, you can learn about these crucial topics and gain the tools you need to take an active role in improving your health now, while you are waiting for the date of your surgery.

Let's start by diving into a real-life story that brings these ideas to life.

Your Journey to Surgery

John had just found out from his doctor that he needed to have knee replacement surgery and had been added to the waiting list. He was a normally positive person, but found he was spending his days in a haze of worry and uncertainty as he waited for his

surgery date. The daunting prospect of undergoing his first big surgical procedure was looming large in his mind, stirring up a mix of fear and nervousness.

He often found himself lying awake at night, replaying his doctor's words and imagining various outcomes. Despite this, he sought solace in the fact that he could take proactive steps to prepare himself physically and mentally for the upcoming procedure.

John often felt isolated; while his friends and family were supportive, they couldn't fully grasp the depth of what he was going through and just how anxious he felt. And not knowing exactly when he was going in for surgery only added to his stress.

If you've been told that you need to have an operation, it's natural to feel anxious or nervous, and to wonder what to expect. It can often be one of the most challenging times we've ever faced. However, with proper preparation and an understanding of the process, you *will* feel more confident and prepared. This book will take you through the general process and supply information and explanations to help deepen your understanding. It is important that you follow all instructions given to you by your healthcare team and ask questions if you're unsure about anything.

You've taken a positive step in your journey to surgery, and you are not alone. At the start of April 2023 there were 7.4 million people in the UK waiting for treatment by the NHS. The situation is similar across the globe, with most healthcare systems affected by service disruptions caused by the COVID pandemic. These have resulted in significant backlogs and patients experiencing long waiting times for surgical procedures and treatment.

In the UK, the median time between listing for surgical intervention and completion of surgery is at a record high. Currently there are over 371,111 UK patients waiting over a year for their treatment and a median waiting time of 13.8 weeks. This is significantly higher than the pre-COVID figure.

Approximately 10% of people who have an operation experience a complication of some sort. This is four times more likely to happen if they are frail or physically inactive before their surgery. Lifestyle interventions and behavioural changes work together to reduce complications, give you better post-surgical outcomes and improve your quality of life, meaning you are better able to live life to the full for longer.

Optimisation for surgery can involve simple measures that can be undertaken by almost anyone, so the waiting list for an operation should really be viewed as a "preparation list'. Using the time spent waiting for a surgical procedure in a productive way can have a hugely positive impact on your outcome. Individuals need to be empowered to make the right choices; however, knowing what is effective can be difficult due to conflicting advice from various sources. The internet and social media are full of contradictory information, and it can be hard to know where to get reputable information.

Currently, we know that, after surgery, 14% of people express some kind of regret about having had their operation. There is no one-size-fits-all way of improving this, as individuals' experiences and feelings can vary widely.

Some of the common reasons behind these regrets are:

Not giving it enough consideration: Patients may regret not having done enough research before undergoing surgery, which could have helped them make a more informed decision or prepare better for their recovery.

Underestimating the recovery process: Patients may not fully understand the amount of time and effort needed for a successful recovery, and may regret not preparing adequately for this process.

Rushing into the decision: Some patients may regret not taking enough time to weigh up the risks and benefits of the operation or explore other treatment options before deciding to undergo surgery.

Unrealistic expectations: Patients may have had elevated expectations of the outcome of their surgery that were not met, leaving them disappointed and regretful.

Experiencing side effects or complications: Some patients may experience unexpected side effects or complications after surgery that they were not prepared for, which can lead to regret and dissatisfaction.

It's important to note that not all patients will experience regret after surgery; most will have positive outcomes and be satisfied with their decision to undergo the procedure. The best way to reduce the risk of regret after surgery is to thoroughly research and understand your procedure, ask questions of the medical team, and have realistic expectations about the potential outcomes and recovery process.

> **When attending appointments with medical professionals, it is often a good idea to take a pre-prepared list of questions. This will help you to avoid the feeling that you missed the chance to get the information you need.**

We want to supply all the information you should consider before undergoing your surgical procedure, so you are confident it is the right decision for you. We want to help you to get fit for your surgery and fit for life afterwards!

Key Takeaways

- ☐ Hearing you need to have an operation can be a worrying experience.
- ☐ It can be hard to know what questions to ask, and how to prepare yourself for surgery.
- ☐ The purpose of this book is to help you find the best way to physically, mentally and emotionally get ready for the operation in the waiting period before it.

Chapter 1

Prehabilitation

"The best preparation for tomorrow is doing your best today."
H. Jackson Brown Jr.

Most of us will be familiar with the concept of rehabilitation, which is defined by the World Health Organisation (WHO) as "a set of interventions designed to optimise functioning and reduce disability in individuals who develop health conditions." The goal of a rehabilitation programme is to help individuals regain their independence, improve their quality of life and return to their usual activities as much as possible AFTER illness, injury or surgery.

Rehabilitation waits until after a significant health event has happened and then aims to get you back to the levels of fitness and day-to-day functioning that you were at before that health event occurred. It aims to restore your physical, mental and emotional functions.

In healthcare we are starting to realise the enormous power of "PREhabilitation". It is about preparation of your body and mind BEFORE a planned health event. Prehabilitation, also known as prehab, refers to a program of exercise, nutrition, and other interventions that is designed to prepare you for an upcoming medical procedure, such as surgery or cancer treatment. If you are due to undergo a surgical procedure then you can prepare yourself for that event through physical, nutritional and psychological support using a prehabilitation programme like the ones detailed in section one of this book.

The goal of prehabilitation is to improve people's physical and emotional health before the procedure, with the aim of reducing the risk of complications and improving the patient's overall outcomes after surgery.

The prehabilitation programmes in this book contain exercise and physical therapy ideas, as well as nutritional plans and stress management techniques. The exercise and physical therapy components include strength and endurance training, flexibility exercises, and breathing exercises. The nutritional plans focus on optimising your diet to promote healing and reduce inflammation, as well as exploring ways to improve your gut microbiome. The stress management techniques include mindfulness practices, relaxation exercises, and access to formal counselling.

And it really works. Let's look at what happened to John.

John's story

The first thing John did was to meet with a dietitian to improve his eating habits. He learned about nutrient-dense foods that could help with wound healing. John started incorporating more lean proteins, fruits, vegetables, and whole grains into his meals.

He also worked on staying hydrated, by drinking more water throughout the day.

Next, John focused on reducing stress. He knew that high stress levels could negatively impact healing, so he made relaxation a priority. He started practising deep breathing exercises, meditation, and yoga a few times a week. These activities helped clear his mind and reduce anxiety about the waiting time for his operation.

John also reached out to friends and family for emotional support. He was open with them about his surgery fears but also made sure they spent quality time together doing fun activities. Their encouragement kept his spirits up.

Adding more physical activity into his routine was another goal. He met with a physical therapist to develop a safe exercise program. They incorporated cardiovascular conditioning, to improve his endurance, along with resistance training, to build strength. Stretching and balance exercises were also important. At the same time, John was mindful to listen to his body and not overdo it.

Getting quality sleep became another focus for John. He established a regular bedtime routine that included winding down without electronics. Using room-darkening shades and a white noise machine helped optimise his sleep environment. On the occasions when John did have trouble sleeping, he sought advice from his doctor.

John also took steps to minimise harmful substances. Though not a smoker, he moderated his occasional alcohol intake and abstained from drinking in the weeks leading up to surgery. John knew that avoiding illicit drugs was essential for his safety during the surgical process.

Throughout his journey, John made self-care a priority. He spent time on hobbies that brought him joy, like photography and woodworking, and made sure to find time for those activities. Practising mindfulness, getting massages, and taking relaxing baths also provided self-care for John.

Finally, John worked on implementing lasting positive changes. He set realistic goals, like doing 10 minutes of strength exercises every day, rather than extreme goals that would be hard to maintain. Rewarding himself for small achievements kept John motivated. He also identified triggers for unhealthy habits and came up with coping strategies.

In the months leading up to John's surgery, he diligently incorporated healthy nutrition, exercise, stress management, social support, and self-care into his routine. He felt empowered taking an active role in his health. Thanks to his dedication to Prehabilitation and lifestyle medicine, John went into surgery feeling his best.

As you read on, you'll learn the exact 'prehab' strategies that John used to feel confident about his recovery, and return to full health in good time afterwards.

The research

Research has shown that prehabilitation can help reduce the risk of complications, improve physical function, and enhance quality of life in patients undergoing surgery or cancer treatment. Prehabilitation is often recommended for patients who are at increased risk of complications due to factors such as age, obesity, or chronic health conditions but can and should be used by everyone.

An alternative way to look at prehabilitation is that it is an element of rehabilitation but your journey to recovery starts prior to surgery. The overarching concept is that you have the power to amend your lifestyle now in ways that will vastly improve your health before a significant event such as an operation. If you do so, you will reduce certain risks from that procedure and improve your chances of an uneventful recovery. It goes back to the old proverb that "prevention is better than cure". If you can prepare yourself for your operation, you can minimise complications. This is so much better for your overall health than just treating any issues that arise after they have happened.

If we look at the world of sports, we see that prehabilitation is widely employed. It is used by sports professionals with one goal in mind: to prevent injuries. A sportsperson spends a huge amount of their time training and preparing for their event and understands that the more time and effort they dedicate to their event preparation, the better the outcome is likely to be.

We can use similar strategies for anyone who is on the waiting list for an operation. Prehabilitation can be used in order to improve an individual's fitness prior to surgery. It can then help them to recover more quickly after their procedure and prevent them from experiencing complications as well as restoring physical function and improves their mental and emotional well-being.

Prehabilitation programmes give you something hugely positive to do while waiting for your surgery. It fills the void between the moment when you are listed for a surgical procedure and when that operation is completed. It helps you to improve your health while you are waiting for your procedure, instead of simply waiting around hoping that things do not get worse.

You are not alone if you are waiting for surgery and have several medical conditions that affect your health and function. These may be things such as high blood pressure, diabetes, coronary artery disease, and arthritis. Lots of people currently on waiting lists for surgery smoke or drink too much alcohol, others live with obesity, and many are frail or physically inactive. These are the very people who will benefit the most from prehabilitation programmes, as they are the ones who are at higher risk of perioperative complications to start with.

> **So why should I take prehabilitation seriously?**
>
> - **Prehabiliation (prehab) is about preparing your body and mind before surgery or treatment, unlike rehabilitation which is after the event.**
> - **Prehab focuses on exercise, nutrition, and psychological support to improve your physical and emotional health prior to surgery or treatment to reduce complications and improve outcomes.**
> - **Prehabilitation is your chance to actively prepare for surgery and improve your recovery journey. It's about taking control of your health journey before the surgery even happens.**

Recovering from surgery

Recovering from surgery can be a gradual process. It requires patience, dedication, and a positive attitude. The specific recovery process will depend on the type of surgery and your overall health and condition. However, there are some general steps that can help promote a smooth recovery after surgery:

Follow your doctor's instructions: It's important to carefully follow any post-operative instructions provided by your doctor and wider healthcare team, including any medications, activity restrictions, and wound care instructions.

Get plenty of rest: Rest is crucial for allowing your body to heal after surgery. Make sure you can get enough sleep and avoid any strenuous activities.

Eat a healthy diet: Eating a nutritious diet can help supply the nutrients your body needs to heal and recover. Focus on eating a wide variety of fruits, vegetables, whole grains, and lean protein sources.

Stay hydrated: Drinking plenty of water and other fluids can help prevent dehydration and promote healing.

Manage pain and discomfort: If you experience pain or discomfort after surgery, talk to your doctor or wider healthcare team about options for pain management, such as medications or physical therapy.

Stay in touch: Attend all scheduled follow-up appointments with your doctor to check your progress and address any concerns or complications.

Gradually increase activity: As you start to feel better, gradually increase your activity levels, as directed by your healthcare team. This can help promote healing and prevent complications.

Be kind to yourself and listen to your body: It can be a frustrating process and you may find your progress involves certain days of feeling better followed by a period of feeling worse again. This is natural, as recovery is non-linear, but try to match your daily activity and goals with how you are feeling that day.

Improving your functional status

Functional status is an important measure of a person's overall health and independence. It can be affected by a wide range of factors, such as age, chronic health conditions, injury, or disability. A person's functional status can also affect their quality of life, ability to work, and social relationships. Functional status refers to an individual's ability to perform activities of daily living (ADLs) and instrumental activities of daily living (IADLs). ADLs include basic self-care tasks, such as washing, dressing, and feeding oneself, while IADLs include more complex tasks such as managing finances, using transport, and performing household tasks.

In healthcare settings, assessing a patient's functional status is important for deciding the right care and interventions, as well as for evaluating the effectiveness of treatments and interventions. Improving an individual's functional status through prehabilitation or other interventions will lead to improved health outcomes and quality of life.

It is important to understand that most patients undergoing surgery will experience a reduction in their functional status in the post-operative period, which is why it is called recovery!

The time it takes for you to return to normal will depend on the nature and extent of the surgical procedure and anaesthetic used, as well as your pre-operative functional status. For someone who has no existing medical conditions who undergoes a minor surgical procedure, it may just be a few hours to recover. We know that, for patients who have a lot of existing medical conditions and undergo major surgery, recovery can be much longer. There is always a chance that they will never regain their normal functional status after their operation.

We also know that patients who experience a complication during or after surgery may experience a slower or incomplete recovery which can threaten their longer-term independence. The good news is that prehabilitated patients are less likely to experience complications and are better placed to regain their normal functioning quicker.

Rupesh's story

Rupesh was a 58-year old accountant who had been waiting over nine months for a knee replacement surgery. After years of worsening osteoarthritis pain, Rupesh was eager to have the surgery and get back to playing golf and tennis.

The long wait had been frustrating for Rupesh. Some days, his knee hurt so much he could barely walk. Other times, it felt a bit better, which made Rupesh second-guess if he even needed the surgery. The uncertainty of when the surgery would happen had been stressing him out.

When Rupesh first got put on the waiting list, he felt there was nothing he could do but wait impatiently. However, after reading

about prehabilitation, Rupesh realised there were many positive steps he could take during this waiting period.

Rupesh started following a prehab program focused on gentle strengthening exercises for his knee, cardiovascular health, and stress reduction techniques. Although it was difficult at first, Rupesh discovered that the more active he stayed, the better his knee felt. His fitness improved, and he also appreciated having a sense of control over his health.

Rupesh is now eagerly looking forward to his knee surgery, knowing his prehab program has got him in the best shape possible. He feels empowered and optimistic about quickly getting back to the activities he enjoys.

Improving your physiological reserve

Physiological reserve refers to the body's ability to respond to and recover from stressors or challenges, such as illness, injury, or ageing. It refers to the body's extra ability or resources that can be used to cope with these stressors. An individual's physiological reserve is a measure of how resilient their body systems are when they are put under physical stress. As part of prehabilitation programmes we aim to build up an individual's physiological reserve.

Examples of physiological reserve include the ability of the heart and lungs to increase their activity during exercise or other physical activity, the ability of the immune system to fight off infections, and the ability of the brain to adapt and recover from injury or trauma.

Physiological reserve is important for supporting overall health and well-being, and for preventing or minimising the impact of age-related decline and disease. However, physiological reserves can decline over time because of factors such as chronic stress, poor diet, lack of physical activity, or chronic disease.

By using a prehabilitation programme like the ones in this book to improve physiological reserve, you may be able to better cope with stressors and maintain your health and independence over time. This is especially important if you have to undergo a surgical procedure or medical treatment. And you will see the benefits of building your physiological reserve before these events.

Consider a time when you are sitting still at rest. Think of all your body functions that keep you alive working together. Now imagine you start doing something physically active like running or jumping. The extra things that your body must do to alter how your body systems are functioning when put under stress contributes to your physiological reserve. The ability of any person to increase the function of their various body systems, when put under stress, relates to an individual's physiological reserve. The more reserve you have, the more able you are to cope with increased physical demands on your body.

The human body is a complex collection of body systems that all work together to keep you alive and well. Oxygen is required by almost every single process in the body. Broadly speaking, the systems work together to bring oxygen into the body via the lungs and then transport that around to all the tissues that require it using your blood vessels. Carbon dioxide is a waste product created by the body; when the oxygen is delivered, the carbon dioxide is collected and transported back to the lungs via blood vessels where we breathe it out.

At times of physical exertion, you need your body to be able to increase your breathing rate and depth so that you get more oxygen into your system, and you can remove the additional carbon dioxide produced because of the increased exertion. You need to increase your heart rate and the blood flow to your muscles and other tissues, so you can deliver that oxygen to where it is needed to facilitate the required level of physical exertion.

It is often said that undergoing major surgery is like running a marathon; in that both are physically demanding, and both require adequate training and preparation. The idea of prehabilitation is that you aim to improve your general health and wellbeing, and change lifestyle risk factors to help you to increase your physiological reserve and bounce back quickly and successfully after surgery. It is the preparation you undertake that gets your body systems ready for the physiological stresses that undergoing a surgical procedure and anaesthesia place on your body. We will discuss the physiological impact surgery has on your body in more detail in section two.

In conclusion, prehabilitation is the practice of enhancing your physiological reserves and day to day functioning before surgery, with the aim of improving your post-operative outcomes.

There is a large and growing body of evidence in the medical literature that effective prehabilitation reduces the time you need to spend in hospital after surgery, reduces the pain experienced after surgery and reduces the chances of having complications from your operation. If you continue the lifestyle changes you make into the post-operative period and beyond, you will also positively affect your longer-term health, help to increase your healthspan and prevent or delay the onset of age-related chronic diseases and disabilities.

Healthspan versus lifespan

> "The key to the future in an ageing society is not found in increasing just our life span; we need to increase our health span at the same time."
>
> Chuck Norris

Healthspan and lifespan are two related but distinct concepts that are often used in discussions of health and ageing. Lifespan refers to the total length of time that an individual is expected to live, based on factors such as genetics, lifestyle, and environmental exposures. It is the amount of time that a person can potentially live but does not necessarily reflect the quality of life and functioning during that time.

Healthspan, on the other hand, refers to the period of life during which an individual is generally healthy, active, and free from chronic disease and disability. It is the quality of life during the time that a person is alive and is a more exact measure of overall health and well-being.

While increasing lifespan has been a major focus of medical research and public health efforts across the globe, increasing healthspan is becoming an increasingly important goal, which can potentially be achieved by following the programmes in this book. By extending the period of life during which people are healthy and able to fully take part in activities, we can help people keep their independence, productivity, and quality of life as they age.

Improving your medical status and fitness before surgery minimises your risks as much as possible. Your healthcare professionals will try to optimise certain health issues such as anaemia, asthma, COPD and blood glucose management before your surgery takes place but there are a lot of things that you can do yourself to become as fit as possible before your surgical procedure.

The good news is that those people who have a lot of comorbidities, and are less physically active now, actually gain the fastest benefits from prehabilitation, so whatever your starting point, there is always something you can do to improve your own outcomes from surgery.

In conclusion, prehabilitation is a proactive approach to prepare your physical and mental health before undergoing surgery or medical treatment. The benefits of prehabilitation are:

- **Improved physical fitness:** Prehabilitation involves exercises and training programs that help to improve a patient's physical fitness, strength, balance, and endurance. This can help to reduce the risk of post-operative complications and speed up the recovery process.
- **Improved mental health:** Prehabilitation can help to improve a patient's mental health by reducing anxiety and stress related to surgery or medical treatment. This can lead to a more positive outlook and faster recovery.
- **Reduced hospital stays:** Patients who undergo prehabilitation are often able to recover faster after surgery or medical treatment, which can result in a shorter hospital stay. This not only reduces the cost of healthcare but also helps to enhance the patient's quality of life.
- **Reduced risk of complications:** Prehabilitation can help to reduce the risk of complications associated with surgery or medical treatment, such as infections, blood clots, and pneumonia. This is

because prehabilitation helps to improve your overall health and immune system.
- **Better outcomes:** Prehabilitation has been shown to positively impact patient outcomes and reduce healthcare costs. Studies have found that patients who undergo prehabilitation have a lower risk of complications and a faster recovery time than those who do not.

Overall, prehabilitation can help to bolster your physical and mental health before you undergo surgery or medical treatment, resulting in a faster recovery, reduced risk of complications, and improved overall outcomes.

Prehabilitation can take a variety of forms and this book will help you to find areas in your own life where you can make significant changes between now and your date of surgery.

You can choose which ones and how you make changes using this book. It guides you through the practicalities of waiting for, undergoing and recovering from surgery and builds in evidence-based lifestyle medicinal practices to help you to get you fit for surgery now and for your life after. We will empower you to optimise your own health to reduce your personal risk of complications and poor outcomes from your surgery. This book will get you fit for surgery and fit for life!

Key Takeaways

- ☐ **Your journey to recovery starts in the period before your operation**
- ☐ **The less fit and active you are currently, the more you have to gain from prehabiiitation**
- ☐ **A positive mindset towards surgery can help foster a positive outcome**

Chapter 2

Pillars of lifestyle medicine

"Well being is as valuable as wealth."

Lailah Gifty Akita

Susan's story

Susan, age 45, had struggled with obesity for most of her adult life. After many failed diets, Susan's doctor suggested bariatric surgery. Susan was hesitant but decided it could be a lifeline. Initially, she had no idea how best to prepare herself for the operation, but after consulting her doctor she chose to undertake a prehab programme.

In the months before surgery, Susan focused on changing her lifestyle habits to prepare herself mentally and physically. She worked with a dietitian to improve her nutrition. Together they planned balanced meals with lean proteins, fruits, vegetables, and whole grains. Susan also began walking daily and taking yoga classes to increase her fitness level.

The prehab program taught Susan mindfulness techniques to manage her stress and relationship with food. She found meditation and journaling helped her cope with difficult emotions without comfort eating. Susan also joined an online bariatric surgery support group.

Although it was challenging at times, Susan embraced the prehab process. She lost 25 lbs before surgery and gained confidence in her ability to make lasting changes. Thanks to her hard work and dedication before surgery, Susan felt empowered about the road ahead.

Lifestyle medicine is an evolving area of clinical practice that looks at ways to prevent, treat, or change non-communicable chronic diseases such as heart disease, obesity and diabetes. These are diseases that are not spread via infection or through other people but are typically caused by unhealthy behaviours. In 2022 they accounted for 71% of deaths that could have been prevented worldwide .

Preparing for surgery can be an important part of ensuring a successful outcome. Making lifestyle changes in the weeks and months leading up to your surgery can help you get in better shape and improve your overall health, making it easier for your body to cope with the stress of surgery and the recovery process that follows.

The pillars of lifestyle medicine are covered in depth in this section, but here is a summary of some potential lifestyle changes that you can make, to get yourself fit for surgery.

Improve your nutrition: Eating a healthy, balanced diet can help boost your immune system and provide your body with the nutrients it needs to heal. Focus on eating plenty of diverse fruits and vegetables, lean proteins, and whole grains, and also limit your intake of processed foods and sugary drinks. Being overweight or obese can increase the risk of complications during and after surgery. If you need to lose weight, focus on making gradual changes to your diet and exercise routine, and aim to lose no more than 0.5-1kg (1-2 pounds) per week.

Optimal nutrition plays a crucial role in preparing your body for surgery and optimising your recovery; we will explore the importance of healthy nutrition and supply practical tips for pre-operative eating habits.

The foods you consume before your surgery significantly affect your body's ability to heal, fight infection, and regain strength. Understanding the specific impact of nutrition on surgery empowers you to make informed choices about your pre-operative diet.

Reduce stress and improve your mental well-being: Stress and anxiety can have a negative impact on your immune system, delay wound healing, and increase the risk of complications during and after surgery. Try to find ways to manage your stress, such as practising relaxation techniques like deep breathing or meditation, or engaging in activities that you find calming and enjoyable.

Maintaining a positive mindset and reducing stress are vital components of preparing yourself mentally for surgery and we will explore various techniques and strategies to enhance your mental wellbeing.

Build healthy relationships: This can help supply emotional support, companionship and a sense of belonging, which can all improve your overall emotional well-being and quality of life. Studies have shown that people with strong, supportive social networks are less likely to experience anxiety, depression, and other mental health issues. There are also physical health benefits from healthy relationships, including a lower risk of stroke and other chronic health conditions.

Nurturing healthy relationships and fostering social connections can supply invaluable support before and after surgery, and we will explore the importance of social interactions and offer guidance on strengthening relationships.

Physical activity: Regular exercise will improve your cardiovascular health, build strength, balance and endurance, and reduce stress. Aim to exercise for at least 20 minutes a day and include a mix of cardiovascular exercise (such as brisk walking, cycling, or swimming) and strength training (such as weightlifting or resistance bands).

Engaging in regular physical activity before surgery can improve your physical fitness and enhance your surgical outcomes and we will explore the benefits of exercise and supply guidance on incorporating physical activity into your pre-operative routine.

Get enough sleep: Getting enough rest is important for your overall health. It can help your body heal after surgery. Sleep plays a crucial role in the body's healing processes and overall well-being. Adequate sleep is essential for physical and mental well-being. Aim for 7-9 hours of sleep per night to ensure optimal recovery and immune system functioning. Create a sleep-friendly environment by keeping your bedroom dark, quiet, and at a comfortable temperature. Practise good sleep hygiene, such as avoiding electronic devices before bed, setting up a relaxing bedtime routine, and avoiding caffeine and stimulating activities close to bedtime. Consider using a sleep tracking device so you can see how changes you make affect your sleep quality.

Quit smoking: Smoking cessation is a crucial step in preparing for surgery and optimising your post-operative recovery. If you smoke, quitting is one of the most important things you can do to prepare for surgery. Smoking can interfere with the healing process, increase the risk of complications during and after surgery, and prolong your recovery time. Smoking has a profound impact on surgical outcomes and the body's ability to heal. Understanding these detrimental effects can serve as a strong motivation to quit smoking before undergoing surgery.

Reduce alcohol: If you are consuming more than 14 units of alcohol per week or regularly drinking more than three alcoholic beverages a day, then moderating your alcohol consumption is essential before surgery to promote a healthy recovery. The impact of excessive alcohol consumption on surgical outcomes is not insignificant; we supply guidance on setting limits according to UK guidelines and discuss the importance of practising responsible drinking.

> **ALCOHOL AND SURGERY**
>
> **We know this may be stating the obvious, but alcohol unfortunately increases your risk of complications from surgery. These can include bleeding, infections and problems with anaesthesia. It can lead to impaired healing and interact with other medications. It is therefore recommended that individuals reduce or avoid alcohol consumption prior to surgery. Aim for two weeks of complete abstinence. Yes, we know that may be hard, but it really will help.**

Avoid illicit drugs: This may be stating the obvious, but avoiding illicit drug use before surgery is crucial for your safety, best surgical outcomes, and overall well-being; we will explore the risks associated with drug use before surgery further, as well as supplying information on seeking help for substance abuse issues in the UK.

Key Takeaways

- ☐ Making lifestyle changes in the weeks and months leading up to your surgery can help you get in better shape and improve your overall health
- ☐ This involves all aspects of your lifestyle, from nutrition and fitness levels, to relationships, and emotional or psychological issues.
- ☐ By making these lifestyle changes, you can improve your overall health and prepare your body for surgery.
- ☐ Be sure to talk to your healthcare team about any specific recommendations or precautions you should take based on your individual health needs and the type of surgery you'll be having.

Chapter 3

Healthy Nutrition

"Let thy food be thy medicine and medicine be thy food!"
                                                    Hippocrates

This chapter is all about fueling your body with healthy nutrition before surgery. It's like prepping your body with the right stuff for a super recovery!

Key Bites:

- Protein, Vitamins, and More: We will explore essential nutrients like protein, vitamins, and omega-3 fatty acids, and where to find them. Think of it as your body's repair kit.
- Balanced Meals: We will offer practical tips for pre-operative eating to ensure you are in the best place on your journey to surgery.
- Stay Hydrated, Stay Happy: Water is your best friend, and we'll tell you why it's so important, especially before surgery.
- We will share our views on intermittent fasting and special diets.

The foods you consume before your surgery can significantly affect your body's ability to heal, fight infection, and regain strength. Understanding the specific impact of nutrition on surgery can empower you to make informed choices about your pre-operative diet.

Certain nutrients play a critical role in supporting the healing process and promoting tissue repair after surgery. These nutrients include:

Protein: Protein is the building block of tissues and is essential for wound healing. Consuming an adequate amount of high-quality protein helps repair damaged tissues, build new cells, and support the immune system. Reliable sources of protein include lean meats, poultry, fish, eggs, dairy products, legumes, nuts, and seeds.

Vitamins and minerals: Various vitamins and minerals are involved in the healing process. Vitamin C is important for collagen synthesis, which strengthens connective tissues. Vitamin A supports cell growth and immunity. Zinc promotes wound healing and helps fight infections. The inclusion of a variety of fruits, vegetables, whole grains, and dairy products in your diet is partly designed to obtain a wide range of vitamins and minerals.

Omega-3 fatty acids: Omega-3 fatty acids have anti-inflammatory properties and thus contribute to reducing inflammation in the body. They can be found in fatty fish like salmon, mackerel, and sardines, as well as in flaxseeds, chia seeds, and walnuts.

Lucy's story

Lucy, 33, had struggled with emotional eating and food addiction issues for years. She would often overeat when stressed, bored, or lonely. Lucy's unhealthy eating habits caused her to develop obesity, high blood pressure, and diabetes. Her doctor said bariatric surgery could be a lifesaving intervention for Lucy.

In the months before surgery, Lucy worked hard on improving her relationship with food through mindful eating practices. She tuned in to her body's natural signals of hunger, fullness, and cravings rather than eating mindlessly. When Lucy felt the urge to overeat, she paused to identify the emotions driving her cravings.

Instead of eating to soothe stress, Lucy went for a walk, called a friend, or wrote in her journal. She stocked her kitchen with nutritious grab-and-go snacks like yoghurt, fruit, and nuts to avoid impulsive unhealthy choices. Lucy also explored new hobbies like painting and reading to fill free time rather than snacking constantly.

Although a daily challenge, Lucy's new mindful eating habits reduced her portion sizes and allowed her to enjoy food more

fully. Lucy felt proud of her hard work and hoped these new skills would support her continued weight and health goals after surgery.

Maintaining a Balanced Diet Before Your Surgery

Maintaining a balanced diet before surgery is crucial. It helps to ensure your body receives all the necessary nutrients. A balanced diet consists of a variety of foods from different food groups, supplying a combination of carbohydrates, proteins, fats, vitamins, and minerals. This helps support your overall health, strengthen your immune system, and optimise your body's ability to heal. A balanced pre-operative diet typically includes:

Fruits and vegetables: These supply essential vitamins, minerals, and antioxidants. Aim for a colourful variety to maximise nutrient intake.

Whole grains: Whole grains such as brown rice, quinoa, whole wheat bread, and oats are rich in fibre, vitamins, and minerals. They supply sustained energy and aid in digestion.

Lean proteins: Choose lean sources of protein, such as poultry (ideally without the skin), fish, tofu, beans, lentils and low-fat dairy products. These help to repair tissues and promote wound healing.

Healthy fats: Include sources of healthy fats in your diet, such as avocados, nuts, seeds, and olive oil. Healthy fats supply energy and support various bodily functions.

Hydration: Staying adequately hydrated is crucial for your overall health as it supports proper bodily functions. Aim to drink plenty of water throughout the day. When you consider that nearly two thirds of your body is water, it becomes clear how important it is to stay well hydrated. Hydration is needed for digestion, for our heart and circulation, for temperature control and for our brain to work well. It is recommended you drink eight glasses of water per day. Checking the colour of your urine is the easiest and most practical way to assess your hydration needs – aim to pass urine which is light yellow to clear in colour. Just keeping a bottle easily accessible during the day usually works best.

There are many reasons to consider intermittent fasting as a healthy lifestyle choice. Whether your goal is to lose weight or simply boost your overall health and vitality, intermittent fasting does not restrict you to specific foods or involve calorie-counting. You simply abstain from eating during fasting hours and eat what you want during eating hours – within reason, of course!

It's this flexibility that makes intermittent fasting so popular, and much easier to adopt as a lasting lifestyle habit. It has become a lifestyle choice for hundreds of people, with many more coming on board as research continues to discover and confirm its seemingly endless benefits.

Whereas health experts had previously warned about the potential dangers of skipping meals, research findings and real-life examples have caused them to do a 180-degree turn. In fact, nutrition experts are now so convinced of the benefits of intermittent fasting that they are now recommending it to clients who simply cannot stick to a traditional diet. More information on how to start and maintain this way of eating is found in the intermittent fasting program later on.

Benefits of intermittent fasting

Studies have proven the powerful and varied benefits of intermittent fasting. Over 75 years of scientific research has conclusively confirmed the following benefits:

- It improves metabolism
- It reduces high blood pressure
- It reduces cholesterol levels
- It promotes longevity
- It reduces oxidative stress
- It improves mental function
- It reduces the risk of age-related degenerative diseases like Parkinson's and Alzheimer's
- It improves insulin sensitivity and can guard against diabetes

- It reduces inflammation
- It reduces the risk of cancer

Who intermittent fasting is not for

Unfortunately, intermittent fasting is not for everyone. There are certain conditions where intermittent fasting can be harmful to health. You must not fast without discussion with a doctor if:

- You are pregnant
- You are breastfeeding
- You are anaemic
- You have a history of disordered eating
- You have diabetes
- You have a heart condition
- You are under 18
- You are on medications that must be taken during meals

Nutritional considerations for specific surgical procedures

Different surgical procedures may have specific nutritional considerations based on the body's increased demand for certain nutrients during the healing process. It is essential to consult with your healthcare team, including your surgeon and a registered dietitian, for personalised dietary recommendations based on your specific surgery.

Orthopaedic surgery: These procedures involve bone, joint, or muscle repair. Calcium, vitamin D, and protein are essential for bone healing and strength.

Gastrointestinal surgery: Procedures that involve the digestive system may require dietary modifications, such as a temporary liquid diet, low residue diets or a low-fibre diet before surgery. Your healthcare team will supply guidance on specific dietary adjustments.

Cardiac surgery: For heart-related procedures, it is essential to follow heart-healthy dietary recommendations that are low in saturated and trans fats, cholesterol, and sodium. Consuming a diet rich in fruits, vegetables, whole grains, and lean proteins that can support cardiovascular health.

In conclusion, understanding the impact of nutrition on surgery empowers you to make informed dietary choices before your procedure. A balanced diet that includes adequate protein, vitamins, minerals, and other essential nutrients supports wound healing, tissue repair, and overall recovery. Always consult with your healthcare team for personalised dietary advice tailored to your specific surgical procedure and individual needs.

Pre-operative dietary recommendations

In addition to understanding the impact of nutrition on surgery, it is essential to follow specific pre-operative dietary recommendations to optimise your body's readiness for the procedure. These recommendations focus on consuming nutrient-dense foods, supporting hydration, and ensuring proper digestion. Here are some practical tips to consider:

Consuming a variety of fruits and vegetables; Fruits and vegetables are rich in vitamins, minerals, antioxidants, and dietary fibre. Aim to include a colourful assortment of fruits and vegetables in your pre-operative diet to provide your body with a wide range of nutrients. Different fruits and vegetables offer unique benefits, so try to incorporate a variety into your meals and snacks.

> **More veggies please!**
>
> **Leafy greens like spinach and kale are excellent sources of vitamins A, C, and K, as well as folate and fibre.**
>
> **Brightly coloured fruits such as berries, citrus fruits and melons are rich in antioxidants and vitamin C.**
>
> **Cruciferous vegetables like broccoli, cauliflower and brussels sprouts have phytochemicals that support immune function.**

Incorporating lean protein sources; Protein is crucial for tissue repair, wound healing, and keeping muscle mass. Include lean sources of protein in your pre-operative meals to support optimal recovery. Choose from:

- Skinless poultry such as chicken or turkey
- Fish and seafood like salmon, tuna, or shrimp
- Legumes such as lentils, chickpeas, or black beans
- Soy products like tofu or tempeh
- Dairy products or dairy alternatives like almond milk

Choosing whole grains: Whole grains supply essential nutrients, fibre, and sustained energy. They can be part of a healthy pre-operative diet and you should opt for whole grain options like:

- Brown rice
- Quinoa
- Whole wheat bread or pasta
- Oats or oatmeal
- Barley

These whole grains offer more fibre, vitamins, and minerals than refined grains, supporting digestion and overall health.

Hydration guidelines and the benefits of staying hydrated

Proper hydration is crucial for supporting overall health and your body's functions. Adequate hydration is especially important before surgery, as it can help prevent complications and promote optimal recovery. Follow these hydration guidelines:

- Drink plenty of water throughout the day, aiming for at least eight glasses (two litres) or more, depending on your activity level and individual needs.
- Limit or avoid sugary beverages, caffeinated drinks, and alcohol, as they can contribute to dehydration.
- If you find it challenging to drink enough water, incorporate hydrating foods like fruits and vegetables with high water content into your diet. Examples include watermelon, cucumbers, oranges, and grapes.

Proper hydration supports digestion, nutrient absorption, circulation, and the elimination of waste products from your body, all of which are important for your overall well-being.

Portion control strategies

Maintaining portion control is crucial, to ensure you are consuming an appropriate amount of calories and nutrients. Overeating can lead to discomfort and potentially interfere with your surgical procedure. If you are prone to overeating, then consider the following portion control strategies:

- Use smaller plates or bowls to visually limit portion sizes.
- Pay attention to your body's hunger and fullness cues. Try to eat slowly and mindfully. Stop eating when you feel comfortably satisfied, rather than overly full.
- Focus on balanced meals that include a combination of lean proteins, whole grains, and a variety of fruits and vegetables.
- Consider collaborating with a registered dietitian who can help you create portion-controlled meal plans tailored to your specific needs.

By following these pre-operative dietary recommendations, you can provide your body with the nutrients it needs for optimal healing and recovery. Remember to consult with your healthcare team, for personalised dietary advice based on your specific surgery and individual requirements.

Dietary restrictions and special considerations

In certain cases, you may have specific dietary restrictions or special considerations to address before your surgery. These restrictions are usually based on your individual health condition, the type of surgery you will undergo, or the medications you are taking. It is important to adhere to these guidelines to minimise potential complications and ensure a smooth surgical process

NBM (Nil by Mouth) guidelines

In many cases, you will receive instructions to avoid eating or drinking for a specified period before your surgery. This is done to reduce the risk of aspiration during anaesthesia and to prepare your digestive system for the procedure. Follow your healthcare team's specific instructions about the duration of fasting, which typically ranges from a few hours to overnight.

During the NBM period, avoid eating any solid foods, including snacks and meals. Refrain from drinking any liquids, including water, tea, coffee, juice, and even clear fluids, as directed by your healthcare team. Your healthcare team may be happy for you to continue drinking small amounts of water during your NBM period, but it is important to check this before you drink any.

You need to adhere strictly to these guidelines to ensure a safe surgical experience. Your healthcare team will provide you with detailed instructions about the specific fasting period for your surgery.

Medication interactions: Some medications can interact with certain foods or supplements, affecting their absorption or effectiveness. Your healthcare team will indicate any medications you should avoid or adjust before surgery. It is important to disclose all medications, including prescription, over the counter and herbal supplements to your healthcare provider.

Medication-related dietary considerations may include:

- Avoiding certain medications that can increase the risk of bleeding, such as blood thinners, before surgery.
- Temporarily stopping the use of specific supplements or herbal remedies that may interfere with anaesthesia or increase the risk of bleeding or other complications.
- Discussing the timing and manner of taking essential medications with your healthcare team to ensure they are optimally absorbed and do not interfere with the surgery.

Follow your healthcare provider's guidance about medication usage and dietary restrictions to ensure a safe and successful surgical experience.

Allergies and food intolerances

If you have known allergies or food intolerances, it is crucial to communicate these to your healthcare team before surgery. Allergies can cause severe reactions that may complicate the surgical process. Your healthcare team will take necessary precautions to avoid exposure to allergens during your procedure.

If you have food intolerances or sensitivities, inform your healthcare team about these as well. They can help accommodate your dietary needs and ensure that you receive proper nutrition before and after surgery.

Pre-operative liquid diets

In some cases, your healthcare team may prescribe a pre-operative liquid diet to help prepare your digestive system for surgery. This is commonly done for procedures involving the gastrointestinal tract. The liquid diet typically consists of clear fluids, such as water, broth, clear juices, and gelatine. Follow your healthcare team's instructions about the duration and specific liquids allowed during this period.

It is important to adhere strictly to the prescribed liquid diet to prevent complications during surgery and ensure a successful outcome.

Individualised recommendations

Depending on your specific health condition, your healthcare team may supply more individualised dietary recommendations before surgery. These recommendations could include:

- Restricting certain foods or beverages that may worsen specific conditions, such as high-sodium foods for individuals with hypertension (high blood pressure) or high-potassium foods for those with kidney disease.

- Changing your diet to manage specific symptoms, such as consuming a low-fibre diet for individuals with gastrointestinal issues or reducing gas-producing foods for those with bloating or gas discomfort.
- Follow your healthcare team's instructions carefully and consult with a registered dietitian if you require further guidance on how to navigate these dietary restrictions or special considerations.

By adhering to the dietary restrictions and special considerations prescribed by your healthcare team, you can ensure a safe and successful surgical experience.

Nutritional supplements and pre-operative optimisation

In addition to following a healthy diet, your healthcare team may recommend specific nutritional supplements to optimise your nutritional status before surgery. These supplements can help address any deficiencies, support immune function, and enhance your body's ability to heal and recover.

Multivitamins and minerals: A multivitamin and mineral supplement can help to ensure that you are receiving a broad spectrum of essential nutrients. This is particularly beneficial if you have dietary restrictions or if your healthcare team finds any nutrient deficiencies. The specific formulation and dosage of the supplement will depend on your individual needs, so consult with your healthcare provider or a registered dietitian for personalised recommendations.

Vitamin C: Vitamin C is a powerful antioxidant that plays a crucial role in collagen synthesis, immune function, and wound healing. It can help promote tissue repair and reduce the risk of infections. Your healthcare team may recommend vitamin C supplementation, especially if you have a higher risk of poor wound healing or if you have a deficiency in this nutrient.

Omega-3 fatty acids: Omega-3 fatty acids, such as those found in fish oil supplements, have anti-inflammatory properties and can support cardiovascular health. They may also aid in reducing inflammation and promoting best healing before and after surgery. Your healthcare team may recommend omega-3 fatty acid supplementation, particularly if you have a diet low in fatty fish or plant-based sources of omega-3s.

Protein supplements: Protein is essential for tissue repair and healing. If your dietary protein intake is insufficient or if you have difficulty meeting your protein needs through food alone, your healthcare team may recommend protein supplements. These supplements can come in various forms, such as powders or ready-to-drink shakes, and can be made from different protein sources, including whey, casein, soy, or plant-based proteins.

Fermented foods: Food that undergo fermentation processes have been shown to improve the diversity of your gut microbiome. Introduce these slowly into your diet and aim to eat a small amount of fermented food such as kimchi, kefir, kombucha or sauerkraut every day.

Probiotics: Probiotics are helpful bacteria that support gut health and immune function. They can encourage a healthy balance of gut bacteria, which is important for proper digestion, absorption of nutrients, and overall well-being. Pre-operative supplementation with probiotics may be recommended, especially if you have gastrointestinal issues or if you will be taking antibiotics before or after surgery.

It is important to note that, while supplements can be beneficial, they should not replace a balanced diet. They are intended to complement a healthy eating plan and address specific nutritional needs. Always consult with your healthcare team or a registered dietitian before starting taking any nutritional supplements, to ensure they are right for you and do not interact with any medications you are taking.

In conclusion, nutritional supplements can be a valuable addition to your pre-operative regimen, helping to optimise your nutritional status and support your body's healing processes. However, they should be used under the guidance of your healthcare team and in conjunction with a healthy diet to ensure the best outcomes for your surgery and recovery.

Key Takeaways

- **A healthy, balanced diet and good hydration are a significant part of any prehabilitation programme**
- **Identify any deficiencies in your diet, and address them through adjusting your diet, or possibly through supplements**
- **Always take the advice of your medical team, especially when it comes to special requirements**

Chapter 4

Mental wellbeing and reduction in stress

"Just when you feel you have no time to relax, know that this is the moment you most need to make time to relax."

Matt Haig

Lucy was a 32-year old schoolteacher waiting for spinal fusion surgery to treat her scoliosis. The surgeon warned her that it could be a lengthy wait.

Initially, Lucy felt anxious thinking about the uncertainty ahead. She worried the long wait would mean worsening pain and disability.

Maintaining a positive mindset and reducing stress are vital components of preparing yourself mentally for surgery. In this chapter, we will explore various techniques and strategies to enhance your mental wellbeing.

Maintaining good mental wellbeing and reducing stress before surgery are crucial for both your emotional and physical health. Elevated levels of stress and anxiety can affect your immune system, delay wound healing, and increase the risk of complications during and after surgery.

Prioritising self-care and seeking emotional support

Taking care of yourself is essential for mental and emotional well-being. Prioritise self-care activities that help you relax, recharge, and reduce stress. Examples of self-care practices include:

> ➢ Adequate rest and sleep: Ensure you are getting enough sleep to support your body's healing processes. Establish a regular

- sleep routine, create a comfortable sleep environment, and practise relaxation techniques before bed.
- Engaging in activities you enjoy: Set aside time for activities that bring you joy and relaxation. This could include reading, listening to podcasts, taking baths, or enjoying hobbies that help you unwind.
- Setting boundaries: Learn to say "no" to added commitments or responsibilities that may cause excessive stress during the pre-operative period. Setting boundaries will allow you to focus on your well-being and reduce unnecessary stressors.

It is essential to reach out for emotional support during the pre-operative period. Share your concerns and feelings with your loved ones, friends, or support groups. Having someone to talk to and offer reassurance can alleviate anxiety and provide a sense of comfort.

Find activities that help you relax and promote a positive mindset. Consider engaging in activities such as:

- Listening to soothing music: Create a playlist of calming music or natural sounds that help you relax and unwind. Listening to pleasant music can have a positive impact on your mood and reduce stress levels.
- Engaging in creative outlets: Explore creative outlets such as painting, writing, or playing a musical instrument. These activities can serve as a form of self-expression and supply a therapeutic escape from stressors.
- Spending time in nature: Spend time outdoors in natural environments, such as parks or gardens. Connecting with nature and being outdoors has been shown to reduce stress, boost your mood, and promote overall well-being.

If you are experiencing persistent anxiety, depression, or other mental health concerns, do not hesitate to seek professional help. Make an appointment to discuss it with your GP. A mental health professional, such as a therapist or counsellor, can supply support, guidance, and proper interventions to help manage your mental well-being before surgery.

Remember, everyone's experience with stress and anxiety differs, so it's important to find the coping strategies that work best for you. Implementing these practices and seeking support can significantly contribute to your mental well-being and reduce stress before your surgery.

Stress management techniques

Engaging in stress management techniques can help alleviate anxiety and promote a sense of calm. Managing stress is crucial for promoting mental well-being before surgery. Here are some expanded explanations of stress management techniques that can help reduce stress and promote a sense of calmness:

Deep breathing exercises are a simple, yet effective way to reduce stress and promote relaxation. By focusing on your breath, you can activate the body's relaxation response and decrease feelings of anxiety. Practise deep breathing exercises to activate the relaxation response. Take slow, deep breaths in through your nose, hold for a few seconds, and exhale slowly through your mouth. Repeat this several times whenever you feel stressed or anxious.

> **BREATHING TECHNIQUES**
>
> **Practise the following deep breathing techniques to help your recovery**
>
> - **Diaphragmatic breathing:** Place one hand on your abdomen and inhale deeply through your nose, allowing your belly to rise. Exhale slowly through your mouth, letting your belly fall. Repeat this pattern, gently focusing on the sensation of your breath.
>
> - **Box breathing:** Inhale deeply for a count of four, hold your breath for a count of four, exhale for a count of four, and hold for a count of four. Repeat this cycle multiple times, visualising a box shape with each breath.

Mindfulness and visualisation techniques

Meditation is another powerful stress management technique that involves focusing your attention and quieting the mind. It can help reduce anxiety and promote a sense of inner calm.

Dedicate a few minutes each day to meditation or mindfulness practice. Find a quiet space, make yourself comfortable, and then focus your attention on the present moment. You can use guided meditation apps or listen to calming music to enhance your relaxation experience.

Mindfulness

Mindfulness involves being fully present in the moment and non-judgmentally viewing your thoughts, sensations, and surroundings. It can help reduce stress and promote mental clarity. Incorporate mindfulness techniques into your daily routine:

- **Body scan meditation: Lie down or sit in a comfortable position, and slowly bring your attention to distinct parts of your body, scanning for any sensations or tension. Allow yourself to relax and release any tension you may feel.**
- **Guided imagery: Engage in guided visualisation exercises, where you imagine yourself in a peaceful and calming environment. Picture yourself in a serene location, such as a beach or forest, and focus on the sensory details, such as the sound of waves or the smell of nature.**

Using yoga and gentle stretching for relaxation

Engage in gentle yoga or stretching exercises to release tension from your body and promote relaxation. Yoga combines physical movements, breathing techniques, and meditation, making it an excellent stress-reducing activity. Engaging in yoga or gentle stretching exercises can help release physical tension and calm the mind.

Consider the following practices:

- **Hatha yoga:** Hatha yoga focuses on gentle poses and slow movements, allowing you to connect with your breath and

release tension. Attend yoga classes or follow online tutorials specifically designed for relaxation and stress reduction.
- ➢ Restorative yoga: Restorative yoga involves using props, such as bolsters and blankets, to support your body in relaxing poses for an extended period. This practice encourages deep relaxation and rejuvenation.

Incorporating hobbies and activities that bring joy and calm

Engaging in activities that bring you joy and calm can be an effective way to manage stress. Dedicate time to hobbies and activities that you enjoy and that promote relaxation.

- ➢ Reading: Set some time aside each day to read books, magazines, or articles that interest you. Reading can transport your mind to different worlds and distract you from stressors.
- ➢ Listening to music: Create a playlist of soothing and calming music that helps you relax. Listen to it during quiet moments or while practising stress management techniques.
- ➢ Spending time in nature: Take walks in natural environments, visit parks, or spend time in your garden. Nature has an ability to calm the mind and can help reduce stress levels.

Remember to prioritise self-care and make time for these stress management techniques. Incorporating them into your daily routine can significantly contribute to reducing stress and promoting a sense of calmness as you prepare for surgery.

Rachel's story

When Rachel expressed her worries to her mother, she gave her daughter some life-changing advice: "Don't just wait for surgery – use this time to help yourself as much as possible."

With renewed optimism, Rachel got creative about using her waiting period in meaningful ways beyond just prehab exercises. She started small, making lists of books she wanted to read and fun DIY projects for around the house.

As an artistic person, Rachels began taking acrylic painting classes and discovered a new passion. She found painting joyful, challenging, and a great stress reliever. It kept her active without straining her back. She also joined an online support group for scoliosis patients, finding comfort in sharing her experience.

Although her back pain limited her at times, she felt empowered, knowing she was being productive. She saw this as precious time to explore new interests and felt hopeful about continuing these pursuits even after surgery.

Key Takeaways

- ☐ Stress and anxiety can damage your body and negatively affect your prehabilitation
- ☐ Find ways to relax and soothe yourself, through hobbies, leisure activities or simply taking time out
- ☐ You mind find practices such as yoga or mindfulness helpful

Chapter 5

Healthy relationships and social connectedness

"The most important things in life are the connections you make with others."

Tom Ford

Nurturing healthy relationships and fostering social connections can supply invaluable support before and after surgery. In this chapter, we will explore the importance of social interactions and offer guidance on strengthening relationships.

Having healthy relationships and supporting social connections is essential for your overall well-being, including your mental and emotional health. Here are some examples and tips for cultivating healthy relationships and enhancing social connectedness before surgery:

Foster open communication: Effective communication is the foundation of healthy relationships. Practise active listening and express your thoughts and feelings openly and honestly with your loved ones. Encourage them to do the same. This can strengthen your bonds and create an atmosphere of trust and understanding.

- Schedule regular check-ins with friends or family members to share updates, thoughts, and emotions.
- Practise active listening by giving your full attention when others are speaking and offering support and validation.

Plan meaningful activities: Engaging in meaningful activities together can deepen your connections with others and create positive memories. Plan activities that align with your shared interests and values, fostering a sense of togetherness and joy.

- Organise a picnic in the park, a hike, or a game night with friends or family members.
- Take part in community events, workshops, or classes that you and your loved ones find interesting.

Show empathy and support: Being empathetic and supportive is crucial in building healthy relationships. Show genuine care and concern for others, offering a listening ear and practical aid when needed. Understand that everyone copes with challenges differently, and your support can make a significant difference.

- Offer to go with a friend or family member to medical appointments or procedures.
- Check in on others regularly to inquire about their well-being and supply emotional support.

Seek supportive communities: Being part of supportive communities or groups can supply a sense of belonging and understanding. Look for communities that share your interests, experiences, or health conditions. These communities can offer emotional support, advice, and a platform for sharing and learning from others' experiences.

- Join online support groups or forums related to your health condition or surgical procedure.
- Engage with local community organisations or clubs that align with your hobbies or interests.

Practice gratitude and appreciation: Expressing gratitude and appreciation can strengthen your relationships and promote positive interactions. Take the time to acknowledge and thank those who support and care for you.

- Write heartfelt thank-you notes or send thoughtful messages expressing your gratitude to friends, family, or healthcare providers.
- Verbally express your appreciation for the support you receive, acknowledging the impact it has on your well-being.

Embrace technology for social connection: In today's digital age, technology offers ways to keep social connections, even when physical distance is a barrier. Embrace the use of video calls, social media, and messaging platforms to stay connected with loved ones.

- Schedule regular video calls with distant family members or friends to catch up and share updates.
- Join online communities or social media groups related to your interests or hobbies, actively engaging in conversations and building connections.

By fostering healthy relationships and nurturing social connections, you create a support system that promotes your well-being before surgery. Remember to communicate openly, engage in meaningful activities, and show empathy and support for others. Utilise technology to stay connected and seek supportive communities that understand and share your experiences. These efforts will contribute to your mental and emotional well-being as you prepare for surgery.

Shazia's story

Shazia dreaded losing her independence after upcoming knee replacement surgery. At 70, living alone with no relatives nearby, she worried about managing basic self-care and household duties during recovery.

Recognizing that social support would be critical, Shazia tried to strengthen her relationships. She reconnected with old friends who could check on her after surgery and help with errands. Shazia's mosque community also coordinated a meal drop-off schedule.

With her neighbour Ruksana , Shazia traded pet-sitting duties and exchanged phone numbers they could call in emergencies. Keeping up with coffee dates at her senior centre gave Shazia social outlets to look forward to.

Shazia found comfort knowing she could rely on her network for help during recovery from the surgery . She felt grateful for the kindness of friends and neighbours as she mentally prepared for this challenging but necessary procedure.

Identifying your support network and their roles

Start by finding the individuals in your life who can serve as a support network during your surgical journey. This network may include family members, friends, neighbours, coworkers, or healthcare professionals. Consider their roles and how they can contribute to your well-being.

- ➢ Family Members: They can offer emotional support, help with daily tasks, and go with you to medical appointments.
- ➢ Friends: They can provide a listening ear, offer encouragement, and help with practical matters, such as meal preparation or transportation.
- ➢ Healthcare Professionals: They can supply guidance, answer medical questions, and coordinate your care.

Reflect on the people in your life who have shown care and support in the past.

Consider the strengths and abilities of each individual and how they can best support you. Communicate your needs and expectations clearly, so everyone understands their roles and can supply the necessary support.

Communicating your needs effectively

Open and honest communication is essential for nurturing healthy relationships and receiving the support you need. Clearly express your needs, emotions, and concerns to your support network, allowing them to understand how they can help you effectively.

- ➢ Be specific about the types of help you may need, such as help with household chores, transportation, or emotional support.
- ➢ Share your fears or anxieties about the upcoming surgery and discuss how your support network can offer comfort and reassurance.
- ➢ Communicate any physical limitations or dietary restrictions you may have after the surgery, so your support network can plan and accommodate your needs.

Practise active listening: Allow others to express their thoughts and concerns.

Use "I" statements to express your feelings and needs, promoting understanding and avoiding blame or judgement, and try to keep lines of communication open and encourage ongoing dialogue throughout your surgical journey.

SUMMARY: HOW TO CREATE YOUR SUPPORT NETWORK FOR SURGERY

Identify your support network

- **Family: Emotional support, help with tasks, and attending appointments**
- **Friends: Listening, encouragement, and practical help**
- **Healthcare Professionals: Medical guidance and care coordination**

Reflecting on your network

- **Consider past support, and align people's strengths with your needs. How can your support network best help you?**

Effective Communication

- **Be specific about the kind of help needed**
- **Share feelings about the surgery**
- **Discuss post-surgery limitations**

Active listening and dialogue

- **Encourage sharing from others**
- **Use "I" statements for feelings**
- **Keep communication open**

You are stronger with the right support. Consult your healthcare provider for more personalised advice.

Engaging with support groups and online communities

Support groups and online communities can supply valuable emotional support, information, and shared experiences. When you connect with individuals who have undergone similar surgeries or faced similar health challenges, it can offer a sense of understanding and encouragement.

> - Join local support groups or organisations that focus on your specific condition or surgery.
> - Explore online forums, social media groups, or dedicated platforms where individuals share their experiences and supply support.

Try to seek out reputable support groups and online communities that prioritise respectful and supportive interactions. Participate actively in discussions, ask questions, and share your experiences to foster connections and receive support.

Remember that every individual's experience and medical condition is unique, so be open to diverse perspectives and approaches.

By building and nurturing your support network, effectively communicating your needs, and engaging with support groups or online communities, you can create a robust support system before and after surgery. Remember to express gratitude for the help and support you receive, as it strengthens the bonds within your relationships.

Strengthening relationships by establishing and respecting boundaries

Building and maintaining healthy relationships is crucial for your emotional well-being and support system before surgery. Establishing and respecting boundaries is essential for supporting healthy relationships. Boundaries define what is acceptable and comfortable for you; they help ensure that your needs are met while respecting the needs of others.

- Clearly communicate your personal boundaries to your loved ones, such as your need for alone time or limitations on physical contact.
- Set boundaries around discussing medical details or your surgical journey, if you prefer to keep that information private.
- Recognise when someone has crossed your boundaries and calmly assert yourself, in order to address the issue.
- Conflict resolution: When conflicts arise, strive for open and honest dialogue, actively listen to the other person's perspective, and work together to find a mutually beneficial solution.

Reflect on your personal values, preferences, and limits to find your boundaries.

Communicate your boundaries assertively and respectfully, using "I" statements to express your needs. Be open to discussing and negotiating boundaries with your loved ones to find a balance that works for everyone.

Practise active listening and avoid interrupting when others are speaking. Choose the right time and place for important conversations to ensure a conducive environment. Seek clarification if you are unsure about someone's intentions or you want to avoid misunderstandings.

Engaging in activities that foster connection and understanding

Engaging in activities that promote connection and understanding can strengthen your relationships and build deeper bonds with your loved ones.
- Quality time: Plan regular activities with your loved ones, such as shared meals, walks, or movie nights; this will help to create opportunities for meaningful interactions and bonding.
- Engaging in mutual interests: Find activities that you both enjoy, such as cooking, gardening, or playing games, to foster shared experiences and strengthen your connection.
- Empathy and support: Practise empathy by actively listening and confirming the feelings and experiences of your loved

- ones. Offer support and encouragement during challenging times.
- Try to prioritise spending regular quality time with your loved ones. Show genuine interest in their lives and actively engage in conversations. Be supportive, and help when needed. And don't hesitate to ask for support yourself.

By building and respecting healthy boundaries, practising effective communication skills, and engaging in activities that foster connection and understanding, you can strengthen your relationships and create a strong support system before surgery.

Remember that relationships require ongoing effort, so take the initiative in keeping lines of communication open and expressing appreciation for your loved ones.

Addressing relationship challenges

Relationships can face challenges and stressors, especially during times of significant change like preparing for surgery. It's important to address these challenges effectively to maintain healthy and supportive relationships. Here are expanded explanations, examples, and tips on addressing relationship challenges:

Coping with conflicts or relationship stressors: Conflicts and stressors are inevitable in any relationship. It's crucial to address them in a constructive and compassionate manner to prevent them from negatively impacting your well-being and the quality of your relationships.

- Open and honest communication: Start a calm and honest conversation to discuss the conflict or stressor, allowing both parties to express their feelings and concerns.
- Active problem-solving: Collaborate with your loved ones to find potential solutions or compromises that address the underlying issues causing the conflict or stress.
- Seeking mediation: If resolving conflicts becomes challenging, consider involving a neutral third party, such as a counsellor or mediator, who can help effective communication and conflict resolution.

Practise active listening and try to understand the other person's perspective, even if you disagree. Use "I" statements to express your feelings and avoid accusatory language. Look for common ground and find mutually beneficial solutions that consider the needs and concerns of all parties involved.

Seeking professional help when necessary: Sometimes, relationship challenges may require professional intervention. Seeking help from a qualified therapist or counsellor can supply valuable guidance and support in navigating complex issues.

- Couples therapy: If the challenges in your relationship persist or become overwhelming, couples therapy can help improve communication, strengthen emotional bonds, and develop effective strategies for problem-solving.
- Individual therapy: If you are personally struggling with relationship challenges or stress, individual therapy can supply a safe space in which to explore your feelings, gain insight, and develop coping strategies.

Recognise when the challenges in your relationship are beyond your ability to resolve independently. Encourage your loved ones to take part in therapy or counselling sessions, emphasising that it's part of a collaborative effort to strengthen the relationship. Research and choose a therapist or counsellor who specialises in relationship issues and has experience working with individuals or couples facing similar challenges.

Remember that seeking professional help is a proactive step towards improving your relationships and overall well-being. Therapists and counsellors can supply valuable tools, perspectives, and strategies to address relationship challenges effectively.

Key takeaways

- ☐ Your social connectedness can play a strong, positive role during your prehabilitation
- ☐ Addressing relationship challenges involves open communication, active problem-solving, and seeking professional help when necessary
- ☐ By proactively addressing conflicts and stressors, you can keep healthy and supportive relationships that contribute to your overall well-being and resilience during the surgical process

Chapter 6

Physical activity

"Health is hearty, health is harmony, health is happiness."

Amit Kalantri

As a chronic smoker with COPD, 55-year-old Nina had become increasingly sedentary over the years. She knew it was crucial to improve her physical fitness before undergoing a lung resection surgery to treat her lung cancer. She had low stamina and feared she lacked the strength for major surgery.

Engaging in regular physical activity before surgery can improve your physical fitness and enhance your surgical outcomes. In this chapter, we will explore the benefits of exercise, and supply guidance on incorporating physical activity into your pre-operative routine. Engaging in regular physical activity before surgery offers numerous benefits that can contribute to improved surgical outcomes.

Strengthening muscles and enhancing cardiovascular health: Regular exercise tones up your muscles and improves cardiovascular health, which can be beneficial before surgery. Strong muscles supply support and stability, aiding in post-operative recovery and reducing the risk of complications. Additionally, improved cardiovascular fitness enhances your body's ability to deliver oxygen and nutrients to tissues, promoting overall health and aiding in the healing process.

- ➢ Resistance training: Incorporate resistance exercises, such as weightlifting or using resistance bands, to target major muscle groups and build strength.
- ➢ - Aerobic exercise: Engage in activities like brisk walking, swimming, or cycling to improve cardiovascular fitness.

Improving flexibility and range of motion: Pre-operative exercise can help improve flexibility and range of motion, which are essential for supporting mobility and preventing muscle stiffness. Increasing flexibility can enhance your ability to perform daily activities and improve your overall physical function.

- ➢ Stretching exercises: Include dynamic and static stretching exercises to improve flexibility. Dynamic stretches involve moving your body through a range of motion, while static stretches involve holding a position to elongate the targeted muscles.
- ➢ Yoga or Pilates: Take part in yoga or Pilates classes to enhance flexibility, balance, and core strength.

Boosting mood and reducing anxiety: Regular physical activity has been shown to have a positive impact on mental health by boosting mood and reducing anxiety. Exercise stimulates the release of endorphins, which are natural mood enhancers. It can also help alleviate stress, improve sleep quality, and enhance overall well-being.

- ➢ Cardiovascular exercises: Engage in activities like running, dancing, or taking part in group fitness classes to elevate your heart rate and release endorphins.
- ➢ Mind-body exercises: Consider practices such as tai chi or qigong, which combine gentle movements, deep breathing, and meditation to promote relaxation and mental well-being.

Incorporating physical activity into your pre-operative routine

When incorporating physical activity into your pre-operative routine, it's important to consider your current fitness level, any limitations or medical conditions, and the recommendations provided by your healthcare team. Here are some tips to help you safely engage in pre-operative exercise:

Consult with your healthcare team: Before starting any exercise program, consult with your healthcare team, including your surgeon and GP. They can supply specific recommendations based on your health condition and the type of surgery you are to undergo.

Start gradually and progress slowly: If you have been sedentary or have limited experience of exercise , start with low-impact activities and gradually increase the intensity and duration. This allows your body to adapt and reduces the risk of injury.

Choose activities you enjoy: Select physical activities that you enjoy as this will increase motivation and adherence. Whether it's walking, swimming, dancing or gardening, find activities that bring you joy or are fun and make it easier to incorporate exercise into your routine.

Listen to your body: Pay attention to your body's signals during exercise. If you experience pain, dizziness, or shortness of breath, take a break and seek medical advice if necessary. Exercise within your comfort level and avoid pushing yourself too hard.

Set realistic goals: Set realistic goals that align with your fitness level and surgical timeline. Break your goals down into individual smaller and achievable milestones to keep yourself motivated and track your progress.

Include a variety of activities: Incorporate a combination of cardiovascular exercises, strength training, flexibility exercises, and balance activities into your routine. This variety helps target different muscle groups and supplies a well-rounded approach to fitness.

Remember, physical activity should be tailored to your individual needs and capabilities. Always prioritise safety and consult with your healthcare team before starting any new exercise program. By incorporating regular physical activity into your pre-operative routine, you can experience the benefits of improved muscle strength, enhanced cardiovascular health, increased flexibility and a boost in mood and overall well-being.

Tailoring an exercise routine

When it comes to physical activity before surgery, it's essential to tailor your exercise routine to your individual needs and capabilities. Before starting any exercise program, it's crucial to consult with your healthcare provider, such as your surgeon, GP, or a physiotherapist.

They can assess your overall health, surgical requirements, and any specific limitations or precautions that need to be considered.

- ➢ Your healthcare provider may recommend specific exercises or activities that are safe and beneficial for your condition or surgery.
- ➢ They can supply guidance on modifications or restrictions based on your unique medical history and current physical condition.
- ➢ If necessary, they may refer you to a physical therapist who can create a tailored exercise program.

Be transparent and provide your healthcare provider with correct information about your medical history, current fitness level, and any concerns you may have. Ask questions to ensure a clear understanding of the recommended exercises and any precautions you need to take. Inform your healthcare provider of any changes in your health or physical condition during your pre-operative period.

Understanding your body

If you have access to a physiotherapist or other fitness expert, they can help you to develop a tailored exercise regime, and also help you to understand your body better. They can explain how various exercises affect the specific muscles, and help you to distinguish the discomfort of exercise from the kind of pain which may be a danger sign.

Setting realistic goals and gradually increasing intensity

When designing your exercise routine, it's important to set realistic goals and gradually increase the intensity and duration of your activities. This approach allows your body to adapt and minimises the risk of injury or excessive strain.

- ➢ Start with shorter exercise sessions and lower intensity activities, such as walking for 10-15 minutes or performing gentle stretching exercises.

- Gradually increase the duration and intensity of your exercises over time. For instance, you can gradually increase your walking time or add light weights to your strength training routine.
- Set specific goals that are achievable and measurable, such as walking a certain distance or performing a certain number of repetitions of an exercise.

Listen to your body and pay attention to any signs of fatigue, pain, or discomfort. Adjust your routine accordingly to prevent overexertion. Celebrate your progress and acknowledge the improvements you make, no matter how small they may seem. If you experience setbacks or challenges, reassess your goals and make necessary adjustments to your routine.

Considering safety

When engaging in physical activity before surgery, it's important to prioritise safety, to prevent injuries and ensure a positive exercise experience. Here are the key considerations to keep in mind.

Warm-up and cool-down techniques: Properly warming up before exercise and cooling down afterward are essential. Warm-up exercises increase blood flow to the muscles, gradually raise your heart rate, and loosen up your joints. Cooling down allows your body to gradually return to its resting state, reducing muscle soreness, and promoting flexibility.

- Warm-up: Before your main exercise session, you can perform light aerobic activities like brisk walking or gentle jogging, followed by dynamic stretching exercises that target the major muscle groups you'll be using.
- Cool-down: After your exercise session, incorporate static stretches that target the muscles you worked on, along with slower-paced movements to gradually lower your heart rate.

Allocate at least 5-10 minutes for both warm-up and cool-down exercises. Focus on dynamic stretches during warm-up, such as arm swings, leg swings, or torso rotations, and hold static stretches for 15-30 seconds during cool-down. Use controlled movements and avoid bouncing or jerking during stretching exercises.

Avoid high-impact activities or movements that may aggravate existing conditions: It's important to choose exercises that are appropriate for your current physical condition and any pre-existing conditions or injuries you may have. Avoid high-impact activities or movements that can place excessive stress on your joints, muscles, or connective tissues.

- ➢ Low-impact cardio: opt for activities like walking, swimming, cycling, or using an elliptical machine, which are gentler on the joints compared to high-impact exercises like running or jumping.
- ➢ Modified movements: If you have specific joint or muscle issues, change exercises to reduce the impact or strain. For example, perform seated leg exercises instead of standing, or use resistance bands instead of heavy weights for strength training.

Listen to your body and avoid activities that cause pain or discomfort. Modify or omit exercises that aggravate existing conditions. Gradually increase the intensity and duration of your exercises over time, allowing your body to adapt and adjust to the demands. If you're unsure about the suitability of certain activities, consult with your healthcare provider or a qualified fitness professional for guidance.

Using proper form and technique: Keeping proper form and technique during exercise is crucial for maximising the benefits and reducing the risk of injury. It ensures that you're targeting the intended muscles and minimising stress on other areas of the body.

- ➢ Strength training: Focus on using controlled movements and keeping proper alignment. For example, when performing a squat, keep your knees aligned with your toes and engage your core muscles.
- ➢ Cardiovascular exercises: Keep good posture and alignment during activities like walking or using cardio machines. Avoid excessive leaning or slouching.

Start with lighter weights or resistance and gradually increase as your form improves and your body adapts. If you're unsure about the correct form or technique for a particular exercise, seek guidance from a qualified fitness professional or use reputable instructional resources. Listen to your body and avoid pushing through pain or sacrificing form for the sake of intensity.

By incorporating warm-up and cool-down techniques, avoiding high-impact activities or movements that may aggravate existing conditions, and using proper form and technique, you can ensure a safe exercise experience before surgery.

Nina's story

Nina started slowly, working with her prehab team to design an exercise plan tailored to her abilities. She began taking short, frequent walks around her neighbourhood, stopping to rest when needed. Nina gradually increased her walking pace and distance over several weeks.

Although difficult at first, Nina persisted through feelings of exhaustion and shortness of breath. She soon noticed improvements - walking became easier, she had less wheezing, and felt more energised overall.

Seeing these positive changes motivated Nina to keep going. By surgery day, she could walk two miles briskly without stopping. Nina felt immense pride in her accomplishments. She knew that preparing her body through exercise would help her recover faster after this life-saving procedure.

Key Takeaways

- ☐ A well-designed exercise routine can be a key element of prehabilitation
- ☐ Whatever your current level of fitness is, you should be able to identify exercises that gradually strengthen your muscles and cardiovascular system
- ☐ Prioritise safety, be mindful of your body's signals, and seek professional guidance when needed
- ☐ Remember, the goal is to improve your physical fitness and prepare your body for the surgical process in the most effective and safe manner possible

Chapter 7

Importance of sleep

"Sleep is the golden chain that ties health and our bodies together."
Thomas Dekker

Adequate sleep is essential for physical and mental well-being; in this section, we will delve into the significance of sleep in the recovery phase before surgery.

Sleep's impact on the immune system and healing processes: During sleep, the body undergoes essential restorative processes that promote healing and support immune function. A sufficient amount of quality sleep enables the body to repair tissues, regenerate cells, and strengthen the immune system, all of which are vital for a successful recovery.

- Tissue repair: Sleep promotes the release of growth hormones, which aid in tissue repair and recovery from injuries or surgical procedures.
- Immune function: Sleep enhances immune system function by increasing the production of immune cells, antibodies, and cytokines that combat infections and support healing.
- Inflammation control: Adequate sleep helps regulate inflammation in the body, reducing excessive inflammation, which can hinder the healing process.

Aim for 7-9 hours of sleep per night to ensure optimal recovery and immune system functioning. Create a sleep-friendly environment by keeping your bedroom dark, quiet, and at a comfortable temperature. Practise good sleep hygiene, such as avoiding electronic devices before bed, setting up a relaxing bedtime routine, and avoiding caffeine after midday as well as stimulating activities close to bedtime.

Importance of setting up a consistent sleep schedule: Keeping a regular sleep schedule is crucial for optimising the quality and duration of your sleep. By adhering to a consistent sleep routine, you can establish healthy sleep patterns and promote better recovery outcomes.

> - Sleep-wake cycles: Consistently going to bed and waking up at the same time each day helps regulate your body's internal clock, promoting a more natural sleep-wake cycle.
> - Sleep efficiency: A regular sleep schedule enhances sleep efficiency, meaning you fall asleep more quickly, experience fewer awakenings during the night, and wake up feeling more refreshed.
> - Circadian rhythm alignment: By aligning your sleep schedule with your body's natural circadian rhythm, you can enhance the quality of your sleep and maximise your body's restorative processes.

Establish a consistent bedtime and wake-up time, even on weekends or days off.

Create a relaxing pre-bedtime routine to signal to your body that it's time to wind down and prepare for sleep. This can include activities like reading, having a warm bath or showers, or practising relaxation techniques. Try to avoid napping excessively during the day, as it can interfere with your ability to fall asleep at night.

By understanding the impact of sleep on the immune system and healing processes and setting up a consistent sleep schedule, you can perfect your recovery and prepare your body for surgery. Prioritise adequate and restful sleep as an integral part of your pre-operative routine to promote optimal physical and mental well-being.

Ray's story

Ray had terrible insomnia in the weeks leading up to his spine surgery. Worrying about potential surgical complications kept Ray awake at night for hours. He was exhausted going into this major procedure.

Ray's prehab doctor suggested improving his sleep hygiene – consistent bedtime routines, limiting devices before bed, etc. But these standard tips didn't address Ray's anxious thoughts keeping him up at night.

Finally, Ray's doctor prescribed a low dose sleeping medication for short-term use. Under medical supervision, the medication helped Ray fall asleep faster without grogginess.

Within a few weeks, Ray broke his cycle of anxious insomnia and established a healthier sleep routine. Getting proper rest left Ray feeling calmer and better equipped, both physically and mentally, to undergo surgery.

Establishing a sleep routine

Creating a consistent sleep routine is essential for promoting quality sleep and maximising your overall well-being before surgery. We will now explore the steps you can take to set up a healthy sleep routine.

Focus on creating a relaxing bedtime routine: A bedtime routine helps signal to your body that it's time to unwind and prepare for sleep. By engaging in calming activities before bed, you can promote relaxation and optimise your chances of falling asleep more easily.

- Avoid using electronic devices: Minimise exposure to devices such as smartphones, tablets, or laptops, for at least an hour before bedtime. The blue light emitted by these devices can interfere with your sleep by suppressing the production of melatonin, a hormone that regulates sleep.
- Set up a wind-down period: Engage in activities that promote relaxation, such as reading a book, listening to soothing music, practising gentle stretching or yoga, taking a warm bath, or practising mindfulness or meditation techniques.
- Create consistency: Perform your bedtime routine in the same order and at approximately the same time each night to establish a consistent pattern that signals to your body that it's time to sleep. Consider using blue-light-blocking glasses in the hours before bed.

Choose activities that you find personally enjoyable and that help you relax and unwind. Experiment with different relaxation techniques to find what works best for you. Be consistent and make your bedtime routine a priority every night.

Creating a sleep-friendly environment: This can significantly enhance the quality of your sleep. By optimising your sleep environment, you can minimise potential disturbances and create a space that promotes restful sleep.

- Darkness: Use blackout curtains or an eye mask to block out external light sources that may disrupt your sleep. Consider using a dim night light if you need to navigate your bedroom during the night.
- Noise control: Use earplugs, a white noise machine, or a fan to mask disruptive noises and create a soothing background sound.
- Temperature and comfort: Keep your bedroom well-ventilated, and at a temperature that is conducive to sleep. Use comfortable bedding, pillows, and mattresses that support your body's needs.

Remove electronic devices and other potential distractions from your bedroom. Make sure your mattress and pillows supply adequate support and comfort. Keep your bedroom clean, organised, and free of clutter to promote a calm and peaceful atmosphere.

Addressing sleep disturbances

If you experience persistent sleep disturbances, such as difficulty falling asleep, frequent awakenings, or daytime sleepiness, it's important to address these issues and seek medical advice if needed. Finding and addressing the underlying causes of sleep disturbances can help improve the quality of your sleep and overall well-being.

Keep a sleep diary to track patterns and find potential triggers or issues affecting your sleep. Maintain open communication with your healthcare provider and discuss any concerns or difficulties you may have with sleep.

By creating a relaxing bedtime routine, perfecting your sleep environment, addressing sleep disturbances, and seeking medical advice, if necessary, you can optimise the crucial role that your sleep plays in your body's healing processes and overall well-being.

Key takeaways

- ☐ Good quality sleep can play a strong, positive role during both your prehabilitation and rehabilitation processes
- ☐ Try to identify the obstacle that are cheating you of sleep and eliminate them
- ☐ Establish a positive routine and environment, to foster good sleep
- ☐ This will also be useful to you during the post-surgery period, as sleep helps the body to heal

Chapter 8

Minimising harmful substances

"The attempt to escape from pain, is what creates more pain."
Gabor Maté

At 35, Sam was diagnosed with oral cancer after years of heavy smoking and tobacco chewing. After the initial shock wore off, Sam realised he needed to quit smoking before the scheduled tumour removal surgery.

Sam had smoked up to a pack a day for over 15 years – the nicotine addiction was intense. He tried quitting cold turkey but couldn't bear the withdrawal. Sam realised he needed help.

Reducing or removing harmful substances from your lifestyle can have a positive impact on your surgical outcomes. In this chapter, we will explore the effects of smoking, excessive alcohol consumption, and illicit drugs, and supply strategies for minimising their use.

Smoking cessation

Smoking cessation is a crucial step in preparing for surgery and optimising your post-operative recovery. There are detrimental effects of smoking that affect your ability to recover from surgical procedures. Smoking has profound negative effects on surgical outcomes and the body's ability to heal. Understanding these detrimental effects can serve as a strong motivation to quit smoking before undergoing surgery.

- Impaired circulation: Smoking damages blood vessels, leading to reduced blood flow to tissues. This hinders the delivery of oxygen and nutrients to surgical sites, impairs wound healing, and increases the risk of complications such as infections or delayed healing.

- Increased risk of infection: Smoking weakens the immune system, making it harder for the body to fight off infections after surgery. Smokers are more susceptible to surgical site infections, pneumonia, and other post-operative complications.
- Respiratory complications: Smoking damages the lungs and reduces lung function, increasing the risk of post-operative respiratory complications such as pneumonia or bronchitis.
- Delayed healing: The nicotine in cigarettes constricts blood vessels, reducing the supply of oxygen and essential nutrients to healing tissues. This can lead to delayed wound healing, prolonged recovery time, and increased risk of complications.

Educate yourself about the specific risks and complications associated with smoking and your planned surgical procedure. This knowledge can reinforce your commitment to quitting. Discuss the importance of smoking cessation with your healthcare provider, who can supply personalised information and guidance based on your specific situation.

Smoking cessation resources and support: Quitting smoking can be challenging, but with the right resources and support, it is possible to overcome this addiction and improve your surgical outcomes. There are various resources available to help you in your journey toward smoking cessation.

- Nicotine Replacement Therapy (NRT): NRT products such as nicotine patches, gums, lozenges, or inhalers can help reduce nicotine cravings and withdrawal symptoms. Consult with your healthcare provider or pharmacist to figure out which NRT option may be suitable for you.
- Medications: There are prescription medications available that can help with smoking cessation by reducing cravings and withdrawal symptoms. Your healthcare provider can guide you in choosing the right medication for your needs.
- Behavioural support: Behavioural support programs, such as counselling, support groups, or smoking cessation helplines, can supply guidance, motivation, and strategies to help you quit smoking. These resources offer emotional support and practical advice on navigating the challenges of quitting.

> Mobile apps and online resources: There are numerous smartphone apps and online platforms designed to aid individuals in their smoking cessation journey. These tools provide tracking mechanisms, personalised support, and access to a community of people with similar goals.

Seek the support of friends, family, and healthcare providers in your efforts to quit smoking. Inform them of your decision and request their understanding and encouragement. Consider joining a support group or attending counselling sessions specifically tailored to smoking cessation. These environments offer a sense of community, accountability, and expert guidance.

It is also good to explore digital resources and mobile apps that offer interactive features, reminders, and progress tracking to help you stay motivated and focused on your goal.

By understanding the detrimental effects of smoking on surgery and recovery, and accessing the available smoking cessation resources and support, you can take proactive steps to quit smoking before your surgery, enhancing your chances of a successful surgical outcome and a healthier future. Remember, quitting smoking is a challenging journey, but the benefits for your overall health and well-being are invaluable.

Sam's story

During his prehab program, Sam enrolled in a smoking cessation counselling program. With support, nicotine gum, and cessation medications, Sam was finally able to kick the habit.

Though it was still a daily struggle, Sam succeeded in quitting smoking just weeks before surgery. Sam knew this major lifestyle change, as hard as it was, would significantly improve his chances of recovering fully from cancer.

Moderating alcohol consumption

If you are consuming more than 14 units of alcohol per week or regularly drinking more than three alcoholic beverages a day, then moderating your alcohol consumption is essential before surgery to promote a healthy recovery. The impact of excessive alcohol consumption on surgical outcomes is significant and here we supply guidance on setting limits according to UK guidelines and discuss the importance of practising responsible drinking. Anything above 14 units is harmful, and it's easy to slip into this without realising.

Setting limits as per UK guidelines and practising responsible drinking: In the United Kingdom, guidelines have been established to promote responsible drinking and reduce the risks associated with alcohol consumption. Adhering to these guidelines is crucial to ensure your overall health and well-being, especially before surgery.

- Moderate drinking: The UK guidelines recommend that neither men nor women should regularly drink more than 14 units of alcohol per week. It is also recommended to spread alcohol consumption evenly throughout the week, avoiding heavy or binge drinking episodes.
- Alcohol-free days: Incorporating alcohol-free days into your week can help reduce overall alcohol intake and promote a healthier relationship with alcohol.
- Pace yourself: When consuming alcohol, pace yourself and aim to have no more than 1-2 standard drinks per hour. This allows your body to metabolise alcohol effectively and reduces the risk of excessive consumption.
- Hydration and alternatives: Alternate alcoholic drinks with water or non-alcoholic beverages to stay hydrated and reduce overall alcohol intake. Choosing alcohol-free alternatives can also be a healthier choice.

Be mindful of your alcohol consumption and track your intake to ensure you stay within the recommended limits. Plan and have non-alcoholic alternatives available during social events or gatherings to reduce the temptation to drink excessively. Seek support from friends, family, or support groups if you find it challenging to moderate your alcohol intake.

Understanding the impact of excessive alcohol consumption on surgical outcomes: Excessive alcohol consumption can have detrimental effects on surgical outcomes and the body's ability to heal. Being aware of these impacts can serve as a motivation to moderate your alcohol intake before undergoing surgery.

- ➢ Impaired healing: Excessive alcohol consumption is proven to interfere with the body's healing processes, leading to delayed wound healing, increased risk of infections, and prolonged recovery time.
- ➢ Increased bleeding risk: Alcohol thins the blood and impairs the body's ability to form blood clots; this can increase the risk of excessive bleeding during and after your surgery.
- ➢ Anaesthesia interactions: Alcohol can interact with anaesthesia medications, leading to complications during surgery.
- ➢ Weakened immune function: Chronic excessive alcohol intake weakens the immune system, making the body more susceptible to infections, impairing the body's ability to fight off post-operative infections, and delaying overall recovery.

Educate yourself about the specific risks and complications associated with excessive alcohol consumption and your planned surgical procedure. This knowledge can reinforce your commitment to moderating your alcohol intake. Discuss the importance of alcohol moderation with your healthcare provider, who can supply personalised information and guidance based on your specific situation.

By understanding the impact of excessive alcohol consumption on surgical outcomes, adhering to UK guidelines for alcohol moderation, and practising responsible drinking habits, you will reduce the potential risks associated with alcohol before surgery and enhance your chances of a successful recovery. Remember, moderation is key, and prioritising your health and well-being should be at the forefront of your choices about alcohol consumption. You should aim to have 14 days of abstinence from alcohol before your procedure.

Stopping illicit drug use

Avoiding illicit drug use before surgery is crucial for your safety, best surgical outcomes, and overall well-being. Here we will explore the risks associated with drug use before surgery, as well as supply information on seeking help for substance abuse issues in the UK.

Risks associated with drug use before surgery: Using illicit drugs before surgery can have severe consequences on your health, surgical outcomes, and recovery process. Understanding these risks can help motivate you to abstain from drug use prior to your surgical procedure.

- Complications during surgery: Illicit drugs can interact with anaesthesia and other medications used during surgery, increasing the risk of adverse reactions, respiratory depression, cardiovascular problems, and other complications during the procedure.
- Impaired healing and recovery: Drug use can hinder the body's natural healing processes, leading to delayed wound healing, increased risk of infections, impaired immune function, and prolonged recovery time.
- Drug interactions and side effects: Illicit drugs can interact with prescribed medications, causing unpredictable reactions and interfering with their efficacy. This can jeopardise your safety before, during and after surgery.
- Increased risk of post-operative complications: Illicit drug use weakens the body's immune system, making you more susceptible to infections, delayed healing, and other post-operative complications.

Educate yourself about the specific risks associated with illicit drug use and your planned surgical procedure. This knowledge can serve as a strong deterrent and reinforce the importance of abstaining from it. Discuss any history of drug use or substance abuse with your healthcare provider, as it is crucial for them to be aware of your health status to provide proper care and support. This is of relevance to your anaesthetist too, so make sure you disclose to them any history of illicit drug use.

Seeking help for substance abuse issues in the UK: If you are struggling with substance abuse issues, it is essential to seek help and support before undergoing surgery. The UK offers various resources and services to individuals who want to overcome substance abuse problems.

> National Health Service (NHS): The NHS provides comprehensive substance abuse services, including counselling, detoxification programs, and rehabilitation facilities. Contact your local NHS trust or general practitioner for guidance and referrals.
> Drug and alcohol helplines: Helplines such as the National Drug Helpline (0800 776 600) and the Frank helpline (0300 123 6600) offer confidential and non-judgmental support, information, and advice for individuals seeking help with substance abuse issues.
> Support Groups: Joining support groups, such as Narcotics Anonymous or local addiction recovery groups, can provide a sense of community, understanding, and ongoing support in your journey towards recovery.

Be honest and open with your healthcare provider about your substance abuse history or concerns. They can supply guidance, refer you to proper resources, and ensure your surgical plan is tailored to your specific needs. Engage in counselling or therapy to address the underlying causes of your substance abuse and develop effective coping strategies. Consider involving your support network, such as trusted friends or family members, in your recovery journey, to provide encouragement and accountability.

Remember, seeking help for substance abuse issues is a courageous step towards a healthier and more fulfilling life. By abstaining from illicit drug use before surgery and reaching out for support, you will improve your overall well-being, enhance surgical outcomes, and pave the way for a successful recovery.

Key takeaways

- ☐ Illicit drug use, smoking, or excessive drinking of alcohol should be avoided during prehabilitation
- ☐ Abusing these substances can have a detrimental effect on surgical outcomes
- ☐ If you are struggling with ceasing or reducing your use of these substances, research their effects on surgical outcomes to strengthen your resolve, and reach out for support if you need it

Chapter 9

Self-care strategies

"Self-care is never a selfish act - it is simply good stewardship of the only gift I have, the gift I was put on earth to offer others."

Parker Palmer

Self-care practices are essential for promoting overall well-being before surgery.

Prioritising self-care is essential for promoting optimal health, well-being, and preparing for surgery. In this section, we will supply guidance on finding your personal self-care needs and preferences.

Self-care involves activities and practices that focus on maximising your physical, mental, and emotional well-being. It is an integral part of keeping a healthy lifestyle and preparing your body and mind for surgery.

- ➢ Stress reduction: Engaging in self-care activities can help reduce stress levels, which is crucial for enhancing your overall health and supporting the healing process.
- ➢ Enhanced resilience: Self-care boosts resilience and equips you with the necessary tools to cope with the challenges associated with surgery, recovery, and life in general.
- ➢ Improved mental health: Prioritising self-care supports your mental health by promoting relaxation, self-compassion, and positive coping mechanisms.
- ➢ Increased energy and vitality: Taking time for self-care replenishes your energy reserves, helping you feel more revitalised, focused, and ready for the demands of surgery.

Understand that self-care is not selfish, but a necessary aspect of supporting overall health and well-being. Acknowledge that your needs may change over time, and it is important to reassess and adjust your self-care practices accordingly. Create a mindset shift that recognises self-care as a long-term investment in your health and quality of life.

Identifying your personal self-care needs and preferences

Self-care is a deeply personal journey, and it is crucial to find and prioritise activities that resonate with you and address your unique needs and preferences.

- Self-reflection: Take time to reflect on activities and practices that bring you joy, relaxation, and a sense of fulfilment. Consider activities you find rejuvenating, whether it's spending time in nature, reading a book, practising a hobby, or engaging in creative pursuits. You can make a list and pin it up somewhere visible in your home as a reminder of what you enjoy.
- Assess your physical needs: Pay attention to your body's signals and find activities that promote physical well-being, such as engaging in regular exercise, eating nourishing meals, getting sufficient rest, and incorporating relaxation techniques like massage or aromatherapy.
- Emotional support: Find sources of emotional support, such as spending quality time with loved ones, seeking therapy or counselling, or joining support groups. Emotional well-being is vital during the pre-operative phase and can also positively impact your recovery journey.

Keep a journal or make a list of self-care activities that resonate with you. Refer to it whenever you need inspiration or a reminder to prioritise self-care. Be open to trying new activities and practices that may enhance your well-being. Explore different self-care options and find what works best for you. Regularly reassess your self-care routine to ensure it continues to meet your evolving needs.

Self-care activities: Engaging in self-care activities is an integral part of preparing for surgery and promoting overall well-being. Self-care activities can promote relaxation, stress reduction, and personal fulfilment.

- ➤ Relaxation techniques: Explore various relaxation techniques, such as deep breathing exercises, meditation, progressive muscle relaxation, or guided imagery. These practices can help calm the mind, reduce stress, and promote a sense of inner peace.
- ➤ Nurturing hobbies and interests: Engage in activities that bring you joy and allow you to immerse yourself in the present moment. This could include hobbies such as painting, gardening, playing a musical instrument, cooking, or practising a sport. Find activities that resonate with you and provide a sense of fulfilment.
- ➤ Mindfulness and self-reflection: Cultivate mindfulness by practising being fully present in the moment and cultivating self-awareness. This can be done through meditation, journaling, or taking mindful walks in nature. Engaging in self-reflection allows you to gain insights, process emotions, and foster personal growth.

Set aside dedicated time each day or week for self-care activities. Prioritise this time and make it non-negotiable. Create a self-care routine that includes a variety of activities to address distinct aspects of your well-being, such as physical, mental, emotional, and spiritual. Customise your self-care activities to align with your personal interests, preferences, and available resources.

Remember, self-care is not a luxury but a necessity for supporting your well-being and preparing for surgery. By recognising the importance of self-care, finding your personal needs and preferences, and engaging in activities that promote relaxation, stress reduction, and personal fulfilment, you can enhance your overall health and well-being before and after surgery.

Lucy's story

In the weeks before spinal surgery, Lucy made a conscious effort to incorporate meaningful self-care activities into her daily routine. She knew reducing stress and nurturing herself would be key to maintaining a positive mindset.

Always an avid gardener, Lucy found solace tending to the plants and flowers in her backyard garden each morning. Caring for the living things that depended on her gave Lucy a sense of purpose during this difficult waiting period, as well as a gentle form of exercise.

Reading also became a form of escape and entertainment for Lucy. She created a cosy space for reading books she'd meant to read for years, losing herself in the pages. On bad pain days, Lucy enjoyed listening to audiobooks while resting in bed.

When socialising with friends became hard, Lucy rekindled her teenage passion for sketching, finding it both meditative and fun. Focusing on simple creative acts like cooking, painting, or writing letters infused the time before surgery with enjoyment.

Immersing herself in the activities she loved helped Lucy relieve stress and maintain a sense of self - which she knew was vital in order to face surgery feeling strong and grounded.

Key takeaways

- ☐ Self-care is not only not selfish, but it is also an indispensable part of prehabilitation
- ☐ Work out which activities you find rejuvenating, meditative, or relaxing, and incorporate them into you daily routine
- ☐ By doing this you will reduce stress and improve your state of mind, which is conducive to a positive health outcome

Chapter 10

Collaborating with practitioners of prehabilitation and lifestyle medicine to implement changes in your behaviour

Collaborating with prehabilitation and lifestyle medicine practitioners can provide you with valuable guidance and support throughout your surgical journey. In this chapter, we will discuss the role of these practitioners and supply tips on finding the right professionals, as making lasting changes in your lifestyle habits requires a strategic approach. These medical professionals can help you in implementing and supporting positive behavioural changes before surgery. By setting realistic goals and employing behaviour modification techniques, you can pave the way for successful long-term change.

Setting realistic goals: Setting realistic goals is a crucial first step in implementing behaviour change. By establishing achievable goals and breaking them down into manageable steps, you increase your chances of success and sustainment.

- ➢ Establishing achievable goals: Set specific, measurable, attainable, relevant, and time-bound (SMART) goals that align with your pre-operative needs and aspirations. For instance, instead of aiming to cut all unhealthy foods, you could set a goal to consume five servings of fruits and vegetables per day.
- ➢ Breaking down goals: Break your goals into smaller, actionable steps. For example, if your goal is to engage in 30 minutes of physical activity daily, you can start by incorporating a 10-minute walk during your lunch break and gradually increase the duration over time.

Be realistic and consider your current capabilities, lifestyle, and resources when setting goals. Setting unattainable goals can lead to frustration and demotivation. Celebrate small milestones along the way, in order to reinforce your progress and keep yourself motivated. Regularly reassess your goals to ensure they still are relevant, and adjust them if necessary.

Behaviour modification techniques: Behaviour modification techniques are effective tools for implementing and keeping positive changes in your habits. By finding triggers, developing coping mechanisms, using positive reinforcement, and creating an environment conducive to healthy habits, you can set up a solid foundation for sustainable change.

- Finding triggers: Pay attention to situations, emotions, or thoughts that may trigger unhealthy behaviours. For example, if stress often leads to emotional eating, find alternative coping mechanisms such as engaging in relaxation techniques, seeking support from loved ones, or practising mindful eating.
- Positive reinforcement: Reward yourself for positive behaviours and achievements along your journey. This can be as simple as acknowledging your efforts, treating yourself to a non-food reward, or keeping a journal to track your progress. Additionally, self-monitoring techniques, such as food and activity logs, can increase self-awareness and accountability.
- Creating an environment conducive to healthy habits: Change your environment to support healthy behaviours. For instance, stock your cupboards with nutritious foods, keep exercise equipment easily accessible, and surround yourself with supportive individuals who share your health goals.

Practice self-compassion and be patient with yourself as you navigate behaviour change. Remember that setbacks are a normal part of the process, and each day is an opportunity to start anew. Seek support from friends, family, or professionals who can supply encouragement, accountability, and guidance throughout your journey. Stay flexible and adapt your strategies as needed. What works for one person may not work for another, so be open to exploring different techniques and approaches.

By setting realistic goals, breaking them down into manageable steps, and employing behaviour modification techniques, you can implement positive changes in your lifestyle before surgery. Remember, change takes time and effort, but with perseverance and the right strategies, you can create lasting habits that contribute to your overall well-being and surgical success.

Key takeaways

- ☐ The medical professionals are not just there to diagnose and medically address your health issues; they are also there to advise you on how best to prepare for and recover from surgery
- ☐ Seek out useful resources and professionals from whom you can get the advice you need to best prepare yourself

Chapter 11

Sample prehabilitation and lifestyle medicine program template and intermittent fasting guide

To aid you in your prehabilitation journey, we have supplied a sample six-week prehabilitation and lifestyle medicine program. It outlines a structured approach to incorporating the principles of prehabilitation and lifestyle medicine into your daily routine. We have also included a guide to intermittent fasting.

These structured plans will guide you through key areas of nutrition, physical activity, stress reduction, sleep, and more, to help you optimise your health and prepare for your upcoming surgery.

Program guidelines

We recommend you follow this program for six consecutive weeks. You should aim to do the activities at least five days per week. The more consistent you are, the better the results will be. It is helpful to check off activities as you complete them and note how you feel. Try to increase intensity and duration of activities slowly over the program. You should speak to your healthcare team if you encounter any problems along the way.

And either way, remember to consult with your healthcare team to tailor these recommendations to your specific needs and circumstances.

Most importantly: be kind to yourself through this process. Change takes time and consistency so make sure you celebrate small wins.

Week 1

Nutrition:
- ➢ Drink eight glasses of water daily.
- ➢ Eat at least two servings of vegetables and two servings of fruit per day.
- ➢ Include lean protein in every meal and snack, such as eggs, chicken, fish, beans, or natural yoghurt.
- ➢ Limit sugary drinks, sweets, fried foods, and processed snacks like chips or cookies to once per week.

Physical Activity:
- ➢ Take a 10-minute walk, on five days this week.
- ➢ Do 8-10 strength training exercises targeting major muscle groups on two days this week. Use light weights or resistance bands.
- ➢ Stretch after your walks and strength sessions, holding each stretch for 20 seconds.
- ➢ Write down your workouts and how they felt.

Stress Reduction:
- ➢ Spend 10 minutes per day doing deep breathing exercises. Inhale deeply through the nose, exhale slowly through the mouth.
- ➢ Try a guided meditation from an app or online video on five days this week. Start with 5-10 minute sessions.
- ➢ Identify two or three stressors and write down positive coping statements for each. For example, "If I feel stressed about my surgery, I will talk to my loved ones or practise deep breathing."

Sleep:
- ➢ Go to bed and wake up at the same time each day. Aim for 7-8 hours per night.
- ➢ Make your bedroom dark, quiet, and cool for optimal sleep.
- ➢ Avoid screens for one hour before bedtime. Read or listen to soothing music instead.
- ➢ Make a note of anything that disturbs your sleep this week.

Week 2

Nutrition:
- ➢ Drink eight glasses of water daily.
- ➢ Eat at least three servings of vegetables and two servings of fruit per day.
- ➢ Include lean protein at breakfast, lunch, and dinner.
- ➢ Limit sugary drinks, sweets, fried foods, and processed snacks to two times this week.

Physical Activity:
- ➢ Take a 15-minute walk on five days this week.
- ➢ Do 10-12 strength training exercises, targeting major muscle groups on two days this week. Increase weights or resistance.
- ➢ Stretch after your walks and strength training, holding stretches for 30 seconds.
- ➢ Note down which exercises felt good. Modify or reduce any that aggravated joints or pain.

Stress Reduction:
- ➢ Spend 15 minutes per day engaging in deep breathing. Try counting to five on each inhale, and five on each exhale.
- ➢ Try a 15-minute guided meditation on five days this week. Consider yoga, body scans, or visualisation.
- ➢ Implement your positive coping statements when you feel stressed. Adjust if needed.
- ➢ Do an activity you enjoy for yourself two times this week – reading, taking a bath, crafting, etc.

Sleep:
- ➢ Maintain your consistent sleep schedule.
- ➢ Make adjustments to your sleep environment if needed – blackout curtains, white noise machine, etc.
- ➢ Limit screen time to 60 minutes before bed and avoid screens in the bedroom if possible.
- ➢ If sleep issues persist, keep a more detailed sleep diary this week. Note bedtime, wake time, quality, disturbances, etc.

Week 3

Nutrition:
- ➢ Drink 8-10 glasses of water daily. Herbal tea and broth can also contribute to fluid intake.
- ➢ Eat four servings of vegetables and three servings of fruit per day. Focus on having a variety of types and colours.
- ➢ Include lean protein with every meal and most snacks. Vary your sources – fish, beans, tofu, eggs, dairy, etc.
- ➢ Limit sugary drinks, sweets, fried foods, and processed snacks to once this week.

Physical Activity:
- ➢ Take a 20-minute walk on five days this week. Incorporate hills or intervals to increase intensity.
- ➢ Do 12-15 strength training exercises targeting major muscle groups, two to three days this week. Lift heavier weights/more resistance.
- ➢ Stretch after exercise for 45-60 seconds per muscle group. Focus on areas for surgery.
- ➢ Add other activities you enjoy like swimming, cycling, dancing, yoga, or other, on one or two days.

Stress Reduction:
- ➢ Spend 20 minutes per day on breathing exercises and meditation. Alternate techniques.
- ➢ Implement coping strategies and positive self-talk when stressed. Reflect on what works best for you.
- ➢ Do activities that bring you joy three times this week – crafts, sports, hobbies, quality time, or others.
- ➢ Share worries or emotions with a loved one or support group. Ask for help if needed.

Sleep:
- ➢ Stick to your consistent sleep routine of 7-8 hours per night.
- ➢ Make your bedroom as dark, quiet, and cool as possible.
- ➢ Limit screen time from one hour before your bedtime. Read, stretch, or take a bath to wind down.
- ➢ If sleep issues continue, consider seeing your doctor for other remedies.

Week 4

Nutrition:
- ➤ Drink 8-10 glasses of water daily. Limit sugary drinks to twice this week.
- ➤ Eat five servings of vegetables and three servings of fruit per day. Focus on leafy greens and berries for antioxidants.
- ➤ Include lean proteins with each meal and snack. Vary your sources.
- ➤ Limit sweets, fried foods, and processed snacks to twice this week.

Physical Activity:
- ➤ Take a 25-minute walk on two days this week.
- ➤ Do 15 strength training exercises targeting all major muscle groups on three days this week. Increase weight/resistance from last week.
- ➤ Stretch all major muscle groups after exercise for 60 seconds each.
- ➤ Add other enjoyable activities like swimming, yoga, cycling etc. 2-3 days this week.

Stress Reduction:
- ➤ Spend 25 minutes per day on meditation, using apps or recordings if you find them helpful.
- ➤ Notice negative thought patterns. Practise positive self-talk and reframing.
- ➤ Engage in a hobby or activity you enjoy every day this week.
- ➤ Reach out to your support network as needed for encouragement.

Sleep:
- ➤ Maintain your set sleep schedule.
- ➤ Optimise sleep hygiene – using an eye mask, ear plugs, or white noise machine as needed.
- ➤ Establish a relaxing pre-bedtime routine like reading or gentle yoga.
- ➤ Avoid caffeinated beverages after noon and minimise liquid intake for two hours before bed.

Week 5

Nutrition:
- ➢ Drink 8-10 glasses of water daily. Limit sugary drinks to once this week.
- ➢ Eat five servings of vegetables and four servings of fruit per day. Focus on a diverse variety and try to eat foods that range across all colours of the rainbow each day.
- ➢ Include protein with every meal and most snacks – eggs, nuts, beans, dairy, meat, or fish.
- ➢ Limit sweets, fried foods, and processed snacks to once this week.

Physical Activity:
- ➢ Take a 30-minute walk on five days this week. Incorporate intervals.
- ➢ Do 15 strength training exercises targeting all major groups on three days this week. Increase weight/intensity from last week.
- ➢ Stretch thoroughly after each workout. Hold stretches for 60-90 seconds.
- ➢ Continue other activities you enjoy, like swimming, yoga, hiking, cycling, dance classes or others on two to three days.

Stress Reduction:
- ➢ Spend 30 minutes per day practising deep breathing, meditation, and guided imagery.
- ➢ Regularly monitor thoughts and reframe negative thinking.
- ➢ Engage in fulfilling hobbies and activities every day.
- ➢ Lean on your social network and ask for help as needed. Attend a local support group meeting.

Sleep:
- ➢ Maintain a set sleep schedule of 7-9 hours per night.
- ➢ Continue optimising sleep environment and hygiene habits.
- ➢ Limit screen time from one hour before bed.
- ➢ If any sleep issues persist, discuss options like cognitive behavioural therapy for insomnia with your doctor.

Week 6

Nutrition:
- ➢ Drink 8-10 glasses of water daily. Avoid sugary drinks.
- ➢ Eat six to seven servings of vegetables and four servings of fruit daily.
- ➢ Include protein with every meal and snack from varied lean sources.
- ➢ Limit sweets, fried foods, and processed snacks to once this week.

Physical Activity:
- ➢ Take 30-minute walks on five days this week.
- ➢ Do 15-20 strength exercises targeting all major muscle groups on three days this week. Progress in terms of weight and intensity.
- ➢ Stretch thoroughly after exercise, holding stretches for 90 seconds.
- ➢ Continue enjoyable activities like swimming, cycling, yoga, etc. 3-4 days this week.

Stress Reduction:
- ➢ Spend 30 minutes per day on breathwork, meditation, guided imagery, or visualisation.
- ➢ Practise positive thinking and gratitude daily.
- ➢ Make time for yourself each day with hobbies, activities, or quality time with loved ones.
- ➢ Attend a local support group meeting. Share your progress and get encouragement.

Sleep:
- ➢ Stick to your set sleep schedule of 7-9 hours per night.
- ➢ Continue optimising your sleep environment and following good sleep hygiene.
- ➢ Limit screen time before bed. Establish relaxing pre-bed routines.
- ➢ If sleep issues persist, consider a sleep study or further medical evaluation.

Great job completing the six-week program! Next, stay consistent with your new healthy habits as you move forward to your surgery date. You've set yourself up for the best possible outcome. We wish you a smooth procedure and speedy recovery.

Intermittent fasting guide

Intermittent fasting requires no complicated preparations, and it is practically cost-free (unless you choose to invest in supplements or special foods). All you need to do is kick start your intermittent fasting routine with these five basic steps.

Step 1: Define your goals

Some people incorrectly assume that the goal of intermittent fasting is to lose weight. But this is by no means the only goal. The first step is to define your personal health goal based on the following categories:

Weight loss: If your primary goal is to shed those extra pounds, then you will have to watch what you eat more carefully than someone who is not looking to lose weight.

You need to keep a closer eye on your food intake – not necessarily by restricting calories, but just by consuming less calorie-rich foods – avoid snacking between meals and perhaps cut out rich desserts. This will optimise your fasting and help you reach your weight loss goal much faster.

Improved mental health and spirituality: Some people fast to improve their mental strength and promote spiritual traits like gratitude, humility, compassion, and learning to accept the simple things in life. If this is true in your case, you would want to eat more "brain foods" to improve your mental focus and cognitive function. To promote spiritual traits, you would perhaps prefer to focus on simple but nutritious meals and incorporate meditation into your fasting plan.

Improve overall health and wellbeing: Some people fast simply to reap all the benefits and to feel healthier and more energised. Fasting, in general, is a great detoxifier of the body; it just leaves you looking better and feeling better. Some of the first benefits you will notice are improved complexion, healthier hair and nails, and more balanced digestion. In this case, you can be more flexible with what you eat, as long as you are focusing on good nutrition. You can also engage in a light outdoor exercise like walking or cycling, or incorporate some other healthy exercise program into your lifestyle.

Step 2: Choose a fasting plan

There are a number of intermittent fasting plans and variations on them, but the following three are the most popular and most commonly practised:

- The 16/8 method
- The 5:2 plan
- The eat-stop-eat plan

The 16/8 method: With this plan, you fast for a full 16 hours, with an eating window of 8 hours every day. Veteran fasters recommend that you start your fast after dinner, around 8pm, and break your fast the next day around noon. You can see why this makes the most sense. You will be less likely to get hungry after a good dinner and seven or eight hours will then be taken up by sleep. Breaking your fast by noon the next day will feel like you are having a late breakfast or brunch. You also have room for a light meal or snack in the late afternoon, before ending your fasting window with a nutritious dinner and repeating the process.

Fluids like water, unsweetened coffee, tea or herbal tea are allowed during fasting hours. In fact, they are highly recommended to keep your body hydrated.

If you're a beginner, this plan may seem overwhelming. However, if you do choose it, you can start with a shorter fasting window of 10 or 12 hours and slowly build up to the full 16 hours.

You can also consider playing around with the times that suit your lifestyle best. For example, if you are an early riser, you can plan to break your fast at 10 am. In this case, your eating window would be until 6 pm. It's just a matter of experimenting a bit and finding the hours that you are most comfortable with.

The 5:2 plan: This method requires you to eat normally for five days of the week then limit your calorie intake to 600–800 calories on the remaining two days. You are not technically fasting on those two days but dividing 600–800 calories over three meals will mean you are drastically limiting your food intake.

No super-restrictive calorie counting is required. Anyone can stay within the required range by using a simple calorie counting app, as well as focusing on low-calorie vegetables and fruits on the two "fasting" days. Which days you fast are totally up to you. Some people prefer to have their fast days back-to-back, for example, Saturday and Sunday. Others prefer to space them out over the week, such as Monday and Thursday. There's no fixed rule here. You decide what works best for your lifestyle and schedule.

The real challenge with this plan is dividing the low-calorie intake over your meals. It would mean consuming an average of 200 calories per meal, which is quite low. Some fasters cut out proteins and carbs on these days and fill up on vegetables and fruits. However, with a little creativity, you can add more variety and eat well on these two days.

The eat-stop-eat plan: The rules of this plan are simple. It involves fasting for a full 24 hours once or twice a week. This means that, if you start fasting at 7pm on Saturday, you consume nothing except liquids until 7pm on Sunday. You eat normally on the other days of the week. This is an excellent natural detox therapy for the body as it gives the digestive system a much-needed rest. However, it's extremely challenging for even veteran fasters, let alone beginners. For this reason, you should not consider jumping in feet first with this plan. It's much better to build up gradually until you feel you're ready for such a challenge.

Step 3: Prepare yourself mentally and know what to expect

If you are an average healthy person with no serious medical condition, intermittent fasting is totally risk-free. Yet, for many people, there is a mental barrier that makes the idea of going without food a little terrifying. The idea of voluntary deprivation is sometimes off-putting. This mental barrier is the real challenge you need to overcome, more than the physical discomfort of fasting itself.

Prepare yourself mentally by understanding that yes, it will be tough, especially at the beginning; but going without food for 12, 16 or even 24 hours will not harm you in any way. In fact, it was the norm for our early ancestors to go without food for long periods of time. As hunters and gatherers, they were sometimes forced to fast until they found food. The human body is totally adapted to fasting.

Keep yourself motivated and mentally tough by keeping your health goals top of mind, as well as the awesome benefits you will gain from fasting. Remember, you are doing it because you care about your health. Try to see it as a new challenge and an exciting adventure you've never tried before. It can actually become a very positive and enjoyable experience.

What to expect: Fasting does have some side effects, at least in the beginning. Being prepared for these will also help toughen you up mentally. The side effects are normal and common, so don't panic if you experience some of the following symptoms:

- Headache
- Drowsiness
- Irritability
- Mood swings
- Brain fog
- Fatigue
- A tendency to overeat and feel bloated when you break your fast
- Constipation
- Obsessing about food
- Hunger pangs

These side effects are perfectly normal, and should subside as your body gradually adapts itself to your new eating method. However, if they don't subside in a couple of weeks, then fasting just may not be for you. In rare cases, intermittent fasting can cause hair loss, sleep disturbances and migraines. Although there is no serious risk involved even with these symptoms, it could be that again, fasting is just nor for you.

Start simple: Another way to prepare yourself physically and mentally is to start with small steps. Rather than choosing an intermittent fasting plan and jumping into it right away, try the following for a week or two until you feel more comfortable with depriving yourself of food.

- Skip breakfast. Have some unsweetened herbal tea or coffee in the morning and don't eat anything else until lunchtime. Do this for one week. It's a great way to ease into the real thing.
- Don't snack. Intermittent fasting can be particularly challenging if you are used to grazing or snacking throughout the day. Prepare yourself by cutting out all snacks between meals for a whole week before starting your fasting plan.
- Don't eat after dinner. Make dinner your absolute final meal of the day. Eat nothing and drink nothing except water, nothing but water until breakfast the next day.

Intermittent fasting can be a mental challenge as well as a physical one. However, it doesn't take long to overcome these hurdles once you get the hang of it. The side effects will gradually disappear, your body will adapt, and you will begin to notice the amazing impact that fasting will have on your health. That will be all the motivation you need to keep going.

Step 4: Nutrition – making every meal count

Whatever your fasting plan, bear in mind that ultimately, you will be eating less. So, applying the "less is more" philosophy is the best way to make fasting work for you. That simply means making the most of what you eat by planning nutrition-packed meals that help you stay more full, more energised and less likely to miss essential nutrients during your fasting hours.

Although intermittent fasting does not involve any food restrictions, it can take a toll on your health if you are filling yourself with fast food and calorie-packed snacks and sweets with zero nutrition. It also defeats the whole purpose of getting fitter and healthier.

By all means, do eat your favourite foods in moderation so that you don't feel deprived. Just make sure to balance them out with a lot of green salads, fresh fruits and other healthy foods.

The great thing about fasting is that almost anything, even your least favourite foods will seem appetising when you're hungry. This creates a terrific opportunity for you to adopt healthier and lasting eating habits by focusing on nutritious options.

Step 5: Organising high-activity and low-activity days

One of the pros of intermittent fasting is that you can easily accommodate it into your lifestyle and schedule. The key is to schedule your fasting on days when you are less active. Here are some tips on how to sail through those fasting days more smoothly.

Schedule 24-hour fasts on weekends: This long fast is not easy, even for veterans. That's why it's best to schedule your 24-hour fasts on weekends when you are able to be less active. You can spend the time in light activities like reading, gardening or even napping so that you conserve more energy.

Exercise on non-fasting days: If you are an athlete or you simply work out regularly, always schedule these intensive exercise days when you are not fasting.

Plan errands for non-fasting days: Try to plan activities like shopping, outings, dentist appointments, etc. on non-fasting days to avoid fatigue.

Accommodate your work schedule to your fasting: If you're lucky enough to be able to do this, you will have a more enjoyable fasting experience. If possible, schedule important meetings and tasks that require more focus and concentration for days when you are not fasting. If you work shifts, again, it's easy to schedule your fasting around them.

If your eating window falls at a time when you are at work, do try to bring a healthy pre-prepared meal from home rather than grabbing something on the go.

This is not to say that you should expect to be walking around like a zombie when you are fasting. In fact, many people report that they are more productive and have more mental clarity when they fast. These are just a few recommendations to help you ease into your fasting days at least in the beginning.

Bear in mind that, despite your planning, there will be those inevitable stressful, chaotic days that come around while you are fasting. Just be mentally prepared for these unexpected emergencies. Hopefully, you will be able to get through them without too much discomfort.

Helpful tips for intermittent fasting

As you are getting into your fasting routine, consider these little tips and tweaks. Most of them are just plain common sense but it's helpful to keep them in mind.

1. If you are a woman, you need to make sure you are taking a good iron supplement. Make sure to get a lot of calcium into your diet as well. Some women may also experience irregular periods due to the hormonal changes caused by intermittent fasting. This is why intermittent fasting is not recommended for women who are trying to conceive.
2. Stay hydrated. It's vital that you remember to drink plenty of water to avoid dehydration while you're fasting . Use your phone alert to remind you to drink a glass of water every hour or so. Water also dulls hunger, so that's an added bonus. Unsweetened herbal tea, hot or cold, is another great alternative. A word of warning here; caffeine does not fall into this category, so don't go overboard on coffee and tea. A cup of unsweetened coffee or tea to perk you up in the morning should really be the limit. If you are unable to take it black, add a few drops of milk or cream.
3. Get into the sun. Sunlight helps regulate the body's circadian rhythm and will help your body cycle adapt to fasting much

faster. Sunlight is also a powerful source of vitamin D. Try to get out into the sun as much as you can. If you are unable to do so, consider a vitamin D supplement.
4. Don't be a hero. Honesty is the best policy when it comes to intermittent fasting. If, after a time, you simply can't function normally and the hunger and discomfort are just too extreme, it's time to call it quits. There's no point in continuing if it feels like torture, or if it is debilitating. It doesn't mean you're weak or that you lack willpower, it just means that, like many other people, your body is just not made for fasting.
5. Eat slowly when you break your fast. The first couple of times you fast, you will tend to be so hungry that you will eat quickly and end up feeling pretty uncomfortable. When you sit down to eat, be mindful of eating slowly and taking small mouthfuls. Don't drink water during the meal. Chew slowly and savour every mouthful so that you avoid feeling bloated and sick after eating.
6. Don't overeat. Remember that, when you break your fast, you will have an extended eating window where you can continue to eat. So, don't do it all at once! Your breakfast should be light and nutritious, and you should stop eating as soon as your hunger is moderately satisfied. Never overfill your stomach, because, after being without food for so long, it will go into overdrive if you overeat. You will feel sluggish, bloated and very uncomfortable indeed.
7. Experiment with different fasting times. Assess your lifestyle, work and family commitments to find the times that are best for you. Experiment with different fasting times before settling on a fasting schedule that suits your high- and low-activity days best.
8. Get a fasting app. Did you know that your phone can play a proactive role in your intermittent fasting? Fasting requires willpower, commitment and sticking to your schedule. A simple fasting app can help you stay on track. A fasting app can do everything from organising your fasting schedule, alerting you to mealtimes, to helping you plan meals and even tracking your weight. There's a great variety of fasting apps available online for free.

9. Keep track of your progress. Tracking your progress is important for keeping you motivated and excited about the changes you will experience. Nutrition experts recommend keeping a good journal. You can use it to record your feelings every few days as well as weight loss and other improvements you start to notice.
10. Enjoy yourself! Intermittent fasting is not a self-imposed punishment. Frankly, if this is the way you perceive it, your chances of making progress are slim. Instead, always look at intermittent fasting as your proactive choice for better health and wellbeing. Your mindset is what creates the line between success and failure.

If you have a positive and enthusiastic mindset, intermittent fasting can become an enjoyable experience.

SECTION 2

Your Journey to Surgery and What to Expect

Chapter 1

The physical effects of having an operation

"A good doctor should not avoid performing surgery or prescribing a bitter pill if it is in the interest of the patient."

Awdhesh Singh

Maria was anxious about having surgery to remove her thyroid gland. At age 42, it would be Maria's first time being put under general anaesthesia. Maria feared potential risks like breathing issues, nausea, and even death.

No matter how small the chances, Maria worried about anaesthesia complications or permanently losing her voice from thyroid surgery. She had trouble sleeping as the surgery date approached, constantly plagued by "what if" thoughts.

The physical effects of surgery can vary depending on the type of surgery and your overall health. In general, surgery is a stressful event that can cause a variety of physiological changes in the body. Some of the common physiological effects of surgery include:

- Stress response: Surgery causes a stress response in the body, which can lead to changes in hormones and metabolism. The stress response can also affect the immune system, making it harder for the body to fight infections.
- Inflammation: Surgery can cause inflammation, which is the body's natural response to injury. Inflammation is a natural process, but it causes redness, swelling and pain, which can lead to discomfort and reduced mobility.
- Fatigue: The body's energy levels may be depleted after surgery, leading to fatigue and weakness.

- Pain: Surgery often causes pain, and managing this after surgery is an important part of the recovery process. Pain can be managed with medications and other therapies, such as physical therapy or acupuncture.
- Healing and recovery: After surgery, the body needs time to heal and recover. This process can take several weeks or months, depending on the type of surgery and your overall health. The body may also need added support during the recovery period, such as physical therapy or rehabilitation.

Categorisation of surgical procedures

It's important to note that these terms are not standardised, and their use can vary among healthcare providers and institutions. Ultimately, you should discuss the urgency, complexity, and risks associated with your surgical procedure with your healthcare team to ensure that you understand the benefits and risks of the procedure as well as any alternative options (including doing nothing).

The terms "minor," "moderate," "major," and "major plus" surgery are often used in the UK and other medical organisations around the world. These terms do not have an agreed definition, but they may be used informally to describe distinct types of surgical procedures based on their complexity, invasiveness, and potential risks.

- **Minor Surgery:** This generally refers to a procedure that can be performed in a relatively short time, under local anaesthesia or sedation, usually in an outpatient setting. Examples include removal of lumps and bumps, biopsies, ear tube insertion, circumcision and simple wound closures.
- **Moderate Surgery:** This may refer to a procedure that requires a longer operative time, may require general or regional anaesthesia, and may require a short hospital stay for recovery. Examples include laparoscopic (keyhole) surgeries, and certain types of plastic surgery.
- **Major Surgery:** This refers to a more complex procedure that requires general or regional anaesthesia, a longer operative time, and a hospital stay for recovery. Examples include major

abdominal or thoracic surgeries, joint replacement surgery, heart surgeries, and neurosurgeries.
- **Major Plus Surgery:** This term is not commonly used, but it may refer to a surgical procedure that is more complex or carries a higher risk of complications than a typical major surgery. Examples could include emergency surgeries, procedures on patients with multiple comorbidities, advanced cancers, or complex trauma injuries.

Minimally invasive surgery

Keyhole surgery, also known as minimally invasive surgery, includes both laparoscopic and robotic assisted surgery. It is a type of surgical technique in which small incisions are made in the body, through which specialised instruments and a tiny camera are inserted.

The camera provides a view of the inside of the body, while the instruments are used to perform the surgery through the small incisions. Keyhole surgery is often used to perform procedures such as gallbladder removal, appendicectomy, hernia repair, prostate removal and many others.

Compared to traditional open surgery, keyhole surgery has several benefits, including smaller incisions, less pain and scarring, shorter recovery times, and a reduced risk of complications. However, not all surgeries can be performed using this technique, and in some cases, open surgery may still be necessary.

Preparing for surgery

Depending on the type of procedure you are having, you may need to undergo pre-operative testing to ensure that you are healthy enough for surgery. This may include blood tests, imaging tests, or other diagnostic tests.

Your surgeon and hospital will provide you with specific pre-operative instructions to follow in the days and weeks leading up to your procedure. This may include dietary restrictions, medication changes, and instructions for preparing your home for your recovery.

The type and extent of activities you may struggle with after an operation depend on several factors, such as the type of surgery, the area of the body involved, and your overall health and fitness level. However, in general, after an operation, you may experience some or all the following difficulties:

Physical activities: Depending on the type of surgery, you may have difficulty with certain physical activities such as walking, climbing stairs, lifting heavy objects, or performing household chores. You may also have a limited range of motion, stiffness, or weakness in the affected area.

Mental activities: You may have difficulty with mental activities such as reading, watching TV, or using the computer. This can be due to factors such as pain, fatigue, or medication side effects.

Fatigue and weakness: It's very common to feel tired and weak after an operation. This can make it difficult to perform activities that require a lot of energy or concentration.

Risks of undergoing surgical procedures

Your healthcare team will evaluate your individual risk factors and take steps to minimise the risks associated with your surgery. It's important to discuss any concerns you may have and to ask your doctor any questions about surgery before deciding to undergo the procedure.

Surgery is a medical procedure that involves cutting into the body to repair or remove damaged or diseased tissue. Although surgery has become safer and more effective with advances in medical technology and techniques, it still carries risks.

Some of the general risks of surgery include:

- Infection: Surgery can introduce pathogens (bugs) into the body, which can lead to infection. Infections can range from mild to life-threatening and may require additional treatment, such as antibiotics or antivirals and possibly further surgery. There is an increased risk of infection in individuals with

weakened immune systems and those who undergo more invasive procedures.
- Bleeding: Surgery involves cutting into the body, which can cause bleeding which can lead to anaemia or other complications. While some bleeding is expected during surgery, excessive bleeding can be dangerous and may require added treatment, such as a blood transfusion or more extensive surgery to stop the bleeding.
- Blood clots: Surgery can increase the risk of blood clots forming in the legs, which can travel to the lungs and cause a pulmonary embolism. Prolonged bed rest and decreased mobility after surgery can increase the risk of blood clots, particularly in individuals with pre-existing clotting disorders. Blood clots can be prevented with medications and by getting up and moving around as soon as possible after surgery.
- Complications with healing: Surgery involves cutting tissues, this requires the body to undertake a healing process. Complications with healing can include poor wound healing, scarring, or the need for more surgeries.

Surgery is generally safe, and millions of people undergo surgical procedures every year without any complications. Surgical procedures are performed by highly trained surgeons and surgical teams who take many precautions to prevent complications, such as using sterile techniques, and administering antibiotics (if indicated) to prevent infections.

The risks associated with surgery have been significantly reduced in recent years thanks to advancements in surgical techniques. Overall, the safety of surgery depends on many factors, including the experience and skill of the surgical team, your medical history and overall health, and the type of procedure being performed.

Risks of anaesthesia

It's important to discuss any concerns you may have about anaesthesia with your anaesthetist before the procedure. They will evaluate your medical history and individual risk factors to help figure out the safest and most appropriate type of anaesthesia for you.

Anaesthesia is an important part of many surgical procedures and is generally considered safe. However, like any procedure, it does carry risks. Some of the potential risks of anaesthesia include:

Allergic reactions: Some people may be allergic to the medications used in anaesthesia, which can cause allergic reactions ranging from mild to severe.

Nausea and vomiting: Anaesthesia sometimes causes nausea and vomiting, which may occur during or after the procedure.

Respiratory problems: Anaesthesia can suppress breathing, and, in some cases, it may be necessary to keep helping with breathing after the procedure.

Cardiovascular problems: Anaesthesia can affect the heart and circulatory system, leading to changes in blood pressure and heart rate which can put strain on the heart.

Post-operative confusion: Some people experience confusion or disorientation after waking up from anaesthesia, which is usually temporary.

Damage to teeth or other structures: In rare cases, anaesthesia can cause damage to teeth, lips, tongue, or other structures in the mouth or throat.

Awareness during surgery: Although incredibly rare, some people may be aware of what is happening during surgery while under anaesthesia.

Neurological problems: Anaesthesia can cause temporary or permanent neurological problems, such as nerve damage, stroke, or paralysis.

Your healthcare team will evaluate your individual risk factors and take steps to minimise the associated risks for you. Anaesthesia is very safe, and millions of people undergo it every year without any complications. The safety of anaesthesia depends on many factors, including the type of procedure, the type of anaesthesia used, and your age, medical history, and overall health.

Anaesthesia is administered and monitored by highly trained healthcare professionals, who work together to ensure your safety during the procedure. They constantly watch your vital signs, such as blood pressure, heart rate, and oxygen levels, and adjust the anaesthesia as needed to keep your comfort and safety.

The risks associated with anaesthesia have been significantly reduced in recent years thanks to advancements in anaesthetic drugs, monitoring technology, and techniques.

Maria's story

As part of Maria's prehab program, her healthcare team provided education about anaesthesia, outlining the procedures to ensure her safety. Maria was relieved to learn how closely the anaesthetic team would be monitoring her vital signs throughout surgery. Her surgeon also discussed all the contingency plans if any issues arose, Maria practised breathing exercises and meditation as part of her prehab routine. This helped lower her anxiety substantially. By the morning of surgery, Maria felt well-prepared thanks to thorough prehab education and stress management tools.

Although still nervous, Maria was able to remain calm and trust her care team.It is important to note that the specific effects of surgery and anaesthesia can vary depending on the type of procedure, individual health status, and other factors. You should discuss any concerns or questions with your healthcare provider before undergoing any surgical procedures.

Healing after surgery

All surgical procedures cause a degree of damage and disruption to our tissues. There may be surgical incisions that we can see but these do not always correlate to the amount of tissue disruption that has occurred as part of the procedure. During healing, the body's energy is redirected towards the healing process, which requires a significant amount of energy, resulting in feelings of tiredness and fatigue. Wound healing is a complex physiological process that involves multiple stages and various types of cells, molecules, and bodily functions. The process of wound healing can be broadly divided into three phases:

Inflammatory Phase: This is the first phase of wound healing, which starts immediately after the injury. This phase is characterised by redness, swelling, and some soreness at the site of injury.

Proliferative Phase: In this phase, new tissue is formed to replace the damaged tissue.

Remodelling Phase: In the final phase of wound healing, the new tissue that was formed in the proliferative phase is remodelled to increase its strength and durability. The newly formed collagen fibres are rearranged and crossed over to improve their strength. This phase can take several months to complete, which is why recovery from a surgical procedure often takes longer than people initially expect.

> **SURGERY REMINDER**
>
> **It may sound obvious, but it's worth repeating. Surgery can be stressful. So listen to your body and do not push yourself too hard, as this can delay your recovery or cause further injury. In most cases, the fatigue will subside as the body continues to heal.**

Numerous factors can affect the process of wound healing, including the severity and size of the wound, the presence of infection or underlying medical conditions, and the patient's overall health and nutrition status. Proper wound care, including cleaning and dressing, can help support the natural process of wound healing and minimise complications.

Practically, while you are recovering from surgery, you may also feel more tired than usual or feel like you can do much less activity before feeling exhausted. This is a common experience; it is generally a result of the body's natural response to surgery and the stress it places on the body during recovery. There are several reasons why you may feel tired after an operation:

The effects of anaesthesia: it can cause grogginess, confusion and drowsiness, which can persist for several hours after the surgery.

Medications: Post-operative medications, such as painkillers, may cause drowsiness or fatigue as a side effect.

Pain and discomfort: Pain and discomfort from the surgery can be physically and emotionally draining, which can contribute to feelings of tiredness and fatigue. Your healthcare team will make sure you have appropriate pain relief after surgery, but you should still expect that things will be a bit sore or uncomfortable afterwards.

Changes in sleep patterns: Sleep patterns may be disrupted after surgery due to pain, discomfort, or changes in routine, which can contribute to feelings of tiredness and fatigue. Being discharged from hospital as early as appropriate and getting back to your own bed can work wonders.

Reduced physical activity: After surgery, individuals may be advised to limit physical activity, which can in turn lead to reduced muscle strength and increased fatigue, meaning individuals must build themselves back up to their pre-procedure strength.

It is important to follow instructions about post-operative care and activity restrictions from the surgeon or medical team. It is also important to listen to your body and not push yourself too hard, as this can delay your recovery or cause further injury. In most cases, the fatigue will subside as the body continues to heal.

Key takeaways

- [ ] It is natural to feel some anxiety before an operation
- [ ] There are some risks associated with surgery, although these will be mitigated as much as possible by your medical team
- [ ] The best way to prepare yourself for the effects of surgery is to ask any questions you have and try to fully understand the process

Chapter 2

The psychological effects of having an operation

"Healing takes courage, and we all have courage, even if we have to dig a little to find it."

Tori Amos

Requiring surgery can have a significant psychological impact on a person. The uncertainty and anticipation of the surgery can cause feelings of anxiety, fear, and stress, which can lead to difficulty sleeping, loss of appetite, and difficulty concentrating.

Some people may also experience a sense of powerlessness and loss of control over their situation, as they may feel that they are at the mercy of the medical system and the scheduling of the surgery. This can lead to feelings of frustration and helplessness, which can further worsen their anxiety and stress.

Additionally, the fear of potential complications or adverse outcomes during the surgery can cause a significant amount of worry and anxiety. This can lead to negative thoughts and feelings, which can be difficult to manage without proper support and resources.

It is important to be aware of the psychological impact of waiting for surgery and to seek support and resources to help manage your emotions and cope with the stress and anxiety that can arise during this time. This may include counselling, support groups, or other interventions to help you feel more in control of your situation and reduce your fears and concerns.

Having surgery can also have a significant psychological impact on a person, both during and after the procedure. The experience of surgery can be traumatic and overwhelming, which can cause a range of emotions such as anxiety, fear, and uncertainty.

During the surgery itself, many people may experience feelings of helplessness and loss of control, as they are unable to actively take part in the process. This can lead to a sense of vulnerability and powerlessness, which can be difficult to manage. Your healthcare professionals will guide you through this process and make it as positive an experience as it can be for you.

After the surgery, patients may experience a range of emotions, including relief that the procedure is over, pain and discomfort, and anxiety about their recovery and the potential for complications. They may also experience feelings of dependency and vulnerability as they rely on others to help with their care and recovery. It is also common to get frustrated if you are not making progress at the rate that you feel you should be, often this is due to unrealistic expectations but if you are concerned you can discuss it with your healthcare team.

Techniques to psychologically prepare yourself for surgery

Waiting for an operation can be psychologically distressing; especially if your operation has been delayed or is a long time ahead. As difficult as it can be, try to keep a positive mindset during this time. If you feel that your psychological welfare is suffering, anxiety is getting on top of you, or you're not coping, contact your GP. You may also be able to refer yourself directly to psychological therapy services. These supply talking therapies for problems such as anxiety, depression and stress.

It's natural to be concerned about your surgery but knowing what's going to happen should help you feel more in control. That's why it's good to ask any questions you have when you see your doctor or nurse.

Breathing techniques, visualisation, distraction, calming music, and nature videos are all techniques that can help you prepare for surgery by reducing anxiety, promoting relaxation, and increasing your sense of control. Here is a brief overview of each techniques:

Breathing techniques: Deep breathing techniques, such as abdominal breathing or box breathing, can help you slow down your breathing and calm your mind. Focus on taking slow, deep breaths, inhaling through your nose and exhaling through your mouth.

Visualisation: This involves imagining a calming scene or situation in your mind, such as a peaceful beach or a mountain retreat. Close your eyes and picture the scene in as much detail as possible, including the sounds, smells, and sensations.

Distraction: Engaging in an activity that requires your attention, such as reading a book or solving a puzzle, can help take your mind off the upcoming surgery and reduce anxiety.

Calming music: Listening to calming music, such as classical music or natural sounds, can help reduce anxiety and promote relaxation. Choose music that you find soothing and calming.

Find a creative activity: This could be painting, practising a musical instrument, dancing, gardening or cooking. Satisfying the more creative side of our brain can help our minds; it can increase your happiness and brain function. Creative activities can also assist people deal with various kinds of trauma and negative feelings by having a calming effect on the brain and body.

In addition to these techniques, follow any pre-operative instructions provided by your doctor to help ensure a successful surgery and recovery.

> **NATURE VIDEOS**
>
> **Watching videos of nature scenes, such as forests, oceans, or waterfalls, can help reduce stress and promote relaxation.**
>
> **Fascinating research from Hong Kong University showed music, mobile apps and elements of nature can alleviate pain and anxiety in post-operative patients. Additionally a study in Turkey, concluded that watching funny and unfunny videos reduces post surgical pain levels.**
>
> **Who knew that YouTube could help us with our surgery and recovery!**
>
> **https://pubmed.ncbi.nlm.nih.gov/32209895/**
>
> **https://www.sciencedirect.com/science/article/abs/pii/S1744388116301542**

Coping with disfiguring surgery

Coping with disfiguring surgery can be a challenging, emotional experience. It is common for individuals to experience a range of emotions, including grief, anger, sadness, and anxiety, as they adjust to their new appearance and learn to live with the physical changes that have occurred to their body.

Here are some coping strategies that may be helpful:

Seek support: Reach out to family and friends for emotional support. It may also be helpful to join a support group where you can connect with others who have undergone similar experiences.

Express your emotions: It is important to allow yourself to feel and express your emotions. Many people find it helpful to keep a journal or talk to a therapist to process your feelings.

Focus on what you can control: Although you may not be able to control the physical changes that have occurred, you can focus on aspects of your life that you can control. This may include setting new goals, learning new skills, or focusing on your relationships.

Practice self-care: Taking care of your physical and emotional health is essential. This may include things from this book such as exercising regularly, eating a healthy diet, getting enough sleep, and engaging in activities that bring you joy and relaxation.

Find meaning: It can be helpful to find meaning and purpose in your experience. This may include volunteering, helping others who are going through similar experiences, or using your experience to advocate for others.

Coping with disfiguring surgery can be a long and challenging process, but with the right support and resources, it is possible to adjust and find a sense of meaning and purpose in your new life.

The impact of your surgery on your family and friends

The impact of having a family member waiting for surgery can also be significant. The uncertainty and anticipation of the surgery often causes family members to experience a range of feelings, including frustration, anxiety, fear, and uncertainty, as they wait for their loved one to undergo the procedure. Family members may also feel a sense of powerlessness and loss of control over the situation, as they may feel that they are not able to do much to help their loved one.

Additionally, family members frequently worry about the potential complications or adverse outcomes during the surgery, which can cause a significant amount of stress and anxiety for them. They may also feel guilty about these thoughts or reluctant to share them with you because they do not wish to add to your worries. It can be a confusing time for everyone, and certainly a time when emotions can be all over the place.

Family members may find information about the surgery and the recovery process helpful, as well as guidance on how to best support their loved one during this time. They may find it useful to find support groups for relatives or find someone to speak to who has looked after a loved one who has had surgery so they know more about what they should expect.

Preparing yourself for having good days and bad days

Non-linear recovery from surgery is a common phenomenon; this is where a patient's recovery does not follow a predictable straightforward path. Instead, it often involves periods of progress, setbacks, and plateaus. This can be due to several factors, such as the type of surgery, the patient's overall health, age, and any complications that may arise.

Some patients may experience rapid improvement straight after surgery, while others may have a slower recovery process. In some cases, patients may experience setbacks or complications, such as infections, bleeding, or other issues that may require more treatment or surgery.

Plateaus are also common in non-linear recovery, where the patient may reach a point where their progress slows or stops. This can be frustrating for patients who expect their recovery to be a steady progression, but it is important to remember that this is a normal part of the healing process. Plateaus can last for days or weeks, but, with patience, continued effort, and proper medical care, your recovery will eventually get back on track.

Patients should follow their doctor's instructions about post-operative care and rehabilitation, and report any unusual symptoms or complications at once. It is also important to maintain a cheerful outlook and stay motivated throughout the recovery process, even during setbacks or plateaus, to help ensure a successful recovery.

Key takeaways

- ☐ There are psychological effects of waiting for surgery, and also the recovery process
- ☐ Listen to your body, and be prepared for the recovery to be an uneven process
- ☐ Use relaxation techniques and other methods to retain a positive outlook

Chapter 3

Using the time before your operation date

The time between the decision that you require an operation and you having the procedure should be viewed as your preparation time, and not simply just as waiting time. It can be frustrating having to wait for procedures, but an understanding of how the system works when it comes to prioritising patients for surgery can be helpful.

How are surgical operations prioritised?

Surgical waiting lists in the UK are prioritised based on clinical need and the urgency of the surgical procedure. The prioritisation system is called the "Validation and Clinical Prioritisation Programme". It is used by healthcare providers to ensure that patients are treated in a timely and appropriate manner, and their waiting lists are prioritised based on individual patient needs.

It assigns patients to one of several priority levels based on their clinical need and the urgency of their surgery. Patients who need urgent surgery, such as those with life-threatening conditions or severe pain, are given the highest priority and are typically seen within a few days or weeks. Patients who need non-urgent surgery, such as those with chronic conditions or mild symptoms, are given a lower priority and may have to wait several months or even years for treatment.

It considers a range of factors when prioritising patients, including the severity and duration of their symptoms, the potential risks and benefits of the surgery, the impact on the patient's quality of life, and the availability of resources and staff.

In addition, some hospitals and healthcare providers may also use other criteria to prioritise surgical waiting lists, such as waiting times, patient age, and comorbidities. This can help explain why you may know of other people waiting for surgery who appear to "jump the queue" and receive their operation before you. It is a complicated system, but ultimately the goal is to ensure that all patients receive the care they need in a timely and efficient manner, while also prioritising those who require more urgent treatment.

In the UK, surgical procedures are further categorised according to their level of urgency. This system is known as the Surgical Triage System or the National Confidential Enquiry into Patient Outcome and Death (NCEPOD) classification. The categorisation system is used to ensure that patients receive proper care based on the urgency of their surgical need.

The categorisation of surgical procedures is based on the clinical urgency and is divided into four categories:

- Emergency: Procedures that need to be performed at once or within hours to save the patient's life or prevent permanent disability. Examples include appendectomy for acute appendicitis, repair of ruptured aortic aneurysm, and treatment of severe traumatic injuries.
- Urgent: Procedures that need to be performed within 24-48 hours to prevent deterioration of the patient's condition. Examples include removal of a non-functioning gallbladder and an obstructed bowel.
- Semi-urgent: Procedures that need to be performed within a few months to prevent the patient's condition from becoming chronic or causing significant morbidity. Examples might include hernia repair.
- Elective: Procedures that can be scheduled in advance, and there is no immediate threat to the patient's health. Examples include cataract surgery, joint replacement surgery and cosmetic procedures.

Reserve lists for surgery

In the context of surgery, a reserve list is a list of patients who require a particular surgery but do not yet have a confirmed date; however, they are available to undergo the procedure if a scheduled patient cancels or cannot undergo the surgery for any reason.

The reserve list serves as a backup for the hospital or clinic, ensuring that there are always patients available to undergo surgery, even if a scheduled patient cancels at the last minute. Patients on the reserve list are typically contacted on short notice and asked to come in for surgery if a spot becomes available.

Reserve lists can be especially important for elective surgeries, which are surgeries that are not urgent or life-threatening. In these cases, patients may be willing to wait for a scheduled surgery date but could benefit from being on the reserve list in case an earlier opportunity arises.

It's important to note that patients on the reserve list should be healthy enough to undergo surgery and already have undergone the necessary medical evaluations and tests to determine their suitability for the procedure. They must also be able to make plans with short notice to be able to come in for their procedure. Speak to your healthcare team to see if they have this kind of system in place.

The logistics of preparing yourself for your surgery

Planning for an operation can be complex and overwhelming, but, by working closely with your healthcare team and following their instructions, you can help ensure a successful outcome.

When preparing for an operation it is useful to consider the logistical aspects, as these are things over which you have some control; making these plans can help you feel better prepared.

Packing for a stay in hospital: It can be helpful to think about what you'll pack to take to hospital with you. You may be given a list, but there are some things most people would need. Things to consider are your regular medication, comfortable clothes and nightwear and any toiletries you need. Don't forget to bring something with you that will help you pass the time, for example, books, magazines, or something to listen to (music/podcasts or audiobooks) using headphones. Ask your hospital about any rules on using mobile phones and don't forget to pack your charger.

Cognitive decline after surgery is a known risk, particularly in older adults or those with pre-existing cognitive impairment. Maintaining good physical health through regular exercise, a healthy diet and adequate sleep can help improve brain function and reduce the risk of cognitive decline. Engaging in any activities that challenge your brain, such as puzzles, or learning a new language or practical skill, can help improve cognitive function and prevent decline.

Studies have shown that reading fiction can increase empathy. One theory is that reading fiction helps us to develop our "theory of mind," which is the ability to understand that others have beliefs, desires, and emotions that may differ from our own. By immersing ourselves in a fictional world and experiencing the thoughts and emotions of characters, we may become better able to understand and empathise with the perspectives of others in real life and increase our own self-compassion and coping strategies.

Dental care: If you have any issues with your teeth or gums like loose teeth or crowns, then it would be helpful to see a dentist before your operation. This can help minimise the risk that your teeth are damaged during your anaesthetic.

Planning your recovery period: It is important to plan for this time and make any necessary arrangements for others to take on any caring duties you have, including for children, elderly relatives and pets. You might need to make some changes at home to help you if you're going to be less mobile for a while after your surgery. You may need to consider the practicalities of your environment and consider moving your favourite chair, or even arranging to sleep downstairs for a while. The NHS can often offer minor adaptations such as handrails or a bath board if this is needed.

It can be helpful to also consider and plan for your post-operative care and recovery time, including who will help you with daily activities, such as washing and dressing, and who will supply transportation home from the hospital and to any follow-up appointments.

Time off work: Depending on the type of procedure you have; you may need to limit your activities during the recovery period. You may need to take time off work. If so, speak to your employer about expected time off, and perhaps plan for a phased return after your operation. It is never an exact science predicting how much time people need off work after a procedure. Do consider that this time may be longer than initially predicted if you encounter a complication.

Driving after an operation: After an operation, it is important to follow the instructions about driving provided by your doctor after the procedure. In general, it is advisable to wait until you are fully recovered and have no pain or discomfort before driving a car. Chapter 8 gives more detailed information on this.

Richard's story

Some people can feel quite isolated in hospital. Close friends and family may find it hard to visit due to limited visiting hours, or physical distance. Richard had to have an urgent back operation during the Covid lockdown, which meant that on top of friends and family living in other parts of the country, his wife and daughter were unable to visit. Before the internet, this would have been a very isolating experience, but fortunately the hospital allowed for usage of mobile phones and laptops, which could be used with headphones. So he was still able to access emotional and psychological support from his social network in the difficult first few days of recovery,

Using the time before your operation date summary

As well as following a prehabilitation plan using the programmes in section two, there are a lot of logistical things you can do to get yourself ready for surgery. It is important to prepare yourself physically and mentally to help ensure the best possible outcome.

Plan: Depending on the procedure and your individual circumstances, you may need to plan transport, childcare, or time off work. Make sure to plan to minimise any stress or disruption caused by your surgery.

Prepare your home: If you will be recovering at home after the procedure, you may need to make some preparations, such as stocking up on groceries, arranging for help with household tasks, or setting up a comfortable recovery area.

Remember, the more prepared you are for your medical procedure, the more likely you are to have a successful outcome.

SELF CHECK - IN

ARE YOU READY FOR SURGERY?

Transport and Support Plan:

- Have you arranged for transportation to and from the hospital?
  - Yes
  - No

- Do you have a plan for any required childcare or pet care during your hospital stay?
  - Yes
  - No

Work and Commitments:

- Have you informed your work and taken the necessary time off for surgery and recovery?
  - Yes
  - No

- Do you have any other commitments or responsibilities you need to delegate or reschedule?
  - Yes
  - No

Home Preparation:

- Have you stocked up on groceries and essentials for your recovery period?

- Yes
- No

- Is your home set up for a comfortable recovery, with necessary items within easy reach?
  - Yes
  - No

Recovery Support:

- Do you have a plan for help with household tasks and personal care if needed post-surgery?
  - Yes
  - No

- Have you arranged follow-up visits or check-ins with your healthcare provider?
  - Yes
  - No

Scoring:

- Mostly Yes: Great! You're well-prepared for your surgery. Keep this momentum going!
- Mostly No: Consider taking some time to address these areas. A bit more planning can help to make your surgery and recovery smoother.

Remember, the more prepared you are for your medical procedure, the more likely you are to have a successful outcome!

Chapter 4

What to expect in the weeks before your operation date

"For surgery, there is a before and an after."

Atul Gawande

Before your operation, you can expect to have several appointments and preparations that are needed to ensure that everything is in place for a successful procedure.

You may have to attend a pre-operative assessment, which will help the healthcare team assess your fitness for surgery and spot any potential risks or complications. During this assessment it is useful to have a list of your current medications including all tablets, gels, pastes, vitamins and supplements you are using and at what doses. If practical, try to know what your current height and weight is as well as the date of your last menstrual period (if applicable).

Pre-operative assessment questionnaires

Pre-operative assessment questionnaires are commonly used before surgery and are a type of medical history form that you are typically asked to complete prior to undergoing surgery. These questionnaires are designed to gather information about your medical history, current health status, and any risk factors that may increase your likelihood of experiencing complications during or after surgery. The information gathered on these questionnaires can help healthcare providers assess your overall health and identify any specific concerns or conditions that may require additional testing or interventions prior to surgery.

Some common components of pre-operative assessment questionnaires may include:

- Medical history: You may be asked to supply information about your past and current medical conditions, as well as any medications you are currently taking.
- Allergies: You will be asked to supply information about any allergies you have to medications or other substances.
- Family history: You may be asked about your family history of medical conditions, such as heart disease, diabetes, or cancer.
- Lifestyle factors: You may be asked about lifestyle factors that may affect your health, such as smoking, vaping, alcohol use, or exercise habits.
- Symptoms: You may be asked about any symptoms you are experiencing, such as shortness of breath, chest pain, or fatigue.
- Surgical history: You may be asked about any previous surgeries you have undergone, including the type of surgery and any complications that occurred.

Pre-operative assessment questionnaires can help healthcare providers find any potential issues that may increase your risk of complications during or after surgery. Depending on the results of the questionnaire, you may be referred for more testing or evaluation prior to surgery, or have your surgical plan adjusted to account for any specific risk factors found. You may also meet with an anaesthetist or pre-operative specialist nurse to discuss anaesthesia options and potential risks.

Pre-operative tests and evaluations

Depending on the nature of your surgery, you may need to undergo other tests or evaluations to assess your overall health and figure out the best approach for your procedure. These may include blood tests, an electrocardiogram (ECG), imaging scans, or other diagnostic tests. There may also be a requirement to undergo screening for various infections such as MRSA, CPE and COVID. This will depend on local policy.

Electrocardiogram: This is a procedure that records the electrical activity of the heart. This test is done by placing small sticky electrodes on the skin of the chest, arms, and legs, which are connected to a machine that records the electrical signals of the heart.

An ECG can detect problems with the heart's rhythm and rate, as well as other conditions such as damage to the heart muscle, poor blood flow to the heart, and the effects of certain medications or medical conditions on the heart.

Cardiopulmonary exercise testing: this is a non-invasive diagnostic test that measures the function of the heart and lungs during exercise. It is commonly used to evaluate patients with symptoms of heart or lung disease, such as shortness of breath, chest pain, or fatigue.

The test involves performing exercise, typically on a stationary bike or treadmill, while connected to various monitoring devices that measure heart rate, blood pressure, and breathing patterns. The test is performed under close supervision by a healthcare provider, who monitors vital signs and symptoms throughout the procedure.

Cardiopulmonary testing (CPET) may be recommended before surgery for patients who are undergoing certain types of surgeries, particularly those that may pose a significant risk to the heart and lungs. The purpose of this testing is to assess your cardiac and pulmonary function during exercise, and to find any underlying conditions that may increase the risk of complications during and after surgery.

Exercise stress test: This procedure requires you to walk on a treadmill or pedal a stationary bike, while your heart rate, blood pressure, and oxygen levels are checked. This test can help figure out how well your heart and lungs function during exercise, and find any signs of heart disease, pulmonary disease, or other conditions that may increase the risk of complications during surgery.

Pulmonary function tests: These tests measure how well your lungs are functioning by assessing lung capacity, airflow, and gas exchange.

Echocardiogram: This test uses ultrasound to produce images of the heart and can help find any structural abnormalities or other conditions that may increase the risk of complications during surgery.

Cardiac stress test: This test involves monitoring the heart's response to stress, typically induced through medication or exercise. It can help find any blockages or other problems with the heart's blood supply.

The results of cardiopulmonary testing can help your healthcare provider decide if any additional interventions, such as medication or supplemental oxygen, are needed to reduce your risk of complications during and after surgery. It can also help guide post-operative care and rehabilitation efforts.

Overall, it's important to follow your doctor's instructions carefully and communicate any concerns or questions you may have. With careful preparation and attention to detail, you can help ensure a safe and successful surgery.

Reviewing medications prior to surgery

Medication adjustments: If you are taking any medications, your doctor may need to adjust your dosage or temporarily stop certain medications in the weeks leading up to your surgery.

It is important to review all your medications with your healthcare provider prior to surgery, including prescription and over-the-counter medications, vitamins, and supplements. Here are some medications that your healthcare provider may want to review or adjust prior to surgery:

Blood thinners: Blood thinners, such as warfarin, clopidogrel, apixaban, rivaroxaban or aspirin, can all increase the risk of bleeding during surgery. Your healthcare provider may adjust the dose or temporarily stop these medications prior to surgery.

Insulin and other diabetes medications: Surgery can affect blood sugar levels, so your healthcare provider may adjust your insulin or other diabetes medications before and after surgery.

Blood pressure medications: Some blood pressure medications can affect heart rate or blood pressure during surgery, so your healthcare provider may adjust the dose or temporarily stop these medications prior to surgery.

Steroids: Long-term use of steroids can affect the body's response to stress during surgery. Your healthcare provider may adjust the dose or temporarily stop these medications prior to surgery.

Anti-inflammatory medications: Nonsteroidal anti-inflammatory drugs (NSAIDs), such as ibuprofen or naproxen, can increase the risk of bleeding during surgery. Your healthcare provider may recommend that you stop taking these medications prior to surgery.

Hormonal medications: If you are taking birth control pills or hormone replacement therapy (HRT) and are scheduled for surgery, it is important to inform your healthcare provider. Your healthcare provider may recommend that you stop taking hormonal medications before surgery to reduce the risk of blood clots. The length of time for which you should stop taking these medications depends on the type of surgery and your individual health status. In general, you may need to stop taking these medications four to six weeks before surgery.

However, it is important to discuss the timing and duration of stopping hormonal medications with your healthcare provider.

After surgery, your healthcare provider may recommend that you wait before resuming hormonal medications. In some cases, you may need to wait several weeks or even months before resuming hormonal medications to minimise your risk of blood clots and other complications.

Supplements: Some supplements, such as garlic, ginkgo biloba, or vitamin E, can increase the risk of bleeding during surgery. Your healthcare provider may recommend that you stop taking these supplements prior to surgery.

It's important to discuss all your medications with your healthcare provider prior to surgery, including any herbal supplements or alternative therapies you may be taking. Your healthcare provider can supply guidance on which medications to continue taking, which to adjust, and which to stop prior to surgery.

> **MEDICATION CHECKLIST**
>
> **As we've said, discuss all medications and supplements with your healthcare provider for personalised advice..**
>
> - **Blood Thinners**
> - **Diabetes Medications**
> - **Blood Pressure Drugs**
> - **Steroids**
> - **NSAID**
> - **Hormonal Medications**
> - **Supplements**

Consenting for surgery

Consenting to your surgery is an important process that involves considering the benefits, risks, alternatives, and the option of doing nothing being discussed with you before you consider your options and decide whether to undergo a surgical procedure.

- *Benefits:* The benefits of the surgery should be explained in detail, including how it will improve your condition or quality of life. This may include a reduction in pain or symptoms, improved mobility or function, or an increased life expectancy or healthspan. It's important to note that, while surgery can be highly beneficial, there are no guarantees, and the outcome of the procedure will vary between individuals.
- *Risks:* It's important to discuss the potential risks and complications of your proposed surgery, which may include bleeding, infection, adverse reactions to anaesthesia, blood clots, or damage to surrounding tissues or organs. The risks vary depending on the type of surgery, your medical history, and other factors. It's important for you to understand these risks and to ask any questions you may have before agreeing to the procedure.
- *Alternatives:* Alternatives to surgery should also be discussed, including non-invasive or minimally invasive options, physical therapy, medication, or lifestyle changes. Depending on your

condition, these alternatives are often as effective or more so than surgery and usually carry fewer risks.
- *Doing nothing:* Finally, the possibility of doing nothing should also be discussed. In some cases, surgery may not be necessary or may not provide significant benefits. You should be fully informed of the consequences of not having surgery and the potential impact on your condition and quality of life.

Once all these elements have been discussed, you should be given time to consider your options and ask any other questions. If you choose to proceed with the surgery, you will need to provide your informed consent, showing that you agree to and understand the risks and benefits of the procedure and want to undergo it.

Overall, the consent process for surgery is important to ensure that you have been fully informed of your options and can make an informed decision about your care.

Requirements for specific types of surgery

Before your surgery, you'll be given specific instructions on how to prepare. These instructions may include avoiding certain medications or supplements and arranging for someone to take you home after your surgery. Your surgeon or healthcare team will also provide you with detailed instructions including guidelines for eating and drinking, bathing, and taking medications.

Your healthcare team may mention specific things you need to undertake as part of the preparation for your procedure. They will explain these in detail, including the practicalities and when these will happen. Here are some of the things that may be needed in certain circumstances.

Pre-operative drinks: Pre-operative drinks are commonly given to patients before surgery to help prepare their body for the upcoming procedure. These drinks are typically clear liquids that are easy to digest and do not leave residue in the digestive tract. The specific type and timing of pre-operative drinks may vary depending on the type of surgery and the preferences of the healthcare provider.

It is important to follow the specific instructions provided by your healthcare provider about these drinks to ensure that your body is properly prepared for the upcoming procedure.

Thromboprophylaxis is the use of medications or other interventions to prevent the formation of blood clots in individuals who are at increased risk of developing deep vein thrombosis (DVT) or pulmonary embolism (PE). Patients undergoing surgery are at increased risk of developing DVT or PE due to factors such as immobilisation, surgical trauma, and inflammation.

Thromboprophylaxis before surgery involves the administration of medications or other interventions to reduce the risk of blood clots forming during or after the surgical procedure. The specific type and timing of thromboprophylaxis will vary depending on the type of surgery, the patient's medical history, and other factors, but some common examples include:

- Anticoagulant medications: Anticoagulant medications, such as heparin, low molecular weight heparin, or fondaparinux, are commonly used to prevent blood clots before surgery. These medications work by inhibiting the clotting factors in the blood, thereby reducing the risk of clot formation.
- Mechanical compression devices: Mechanical compression devices, such as compression stockings or pneumatic compression boots, may be used to improve blood flow in the legs and reduce the risk of DVT or PE.
- Early mobilisation: Patients may be encouraged to move around as soon as possible after surgery to promote blood flow and reduce the risk of blood clots.

It is important to follow the specific instructions provided by your healthcare provider regarding thromboprophylaxis before surgery to ensure that you are properly protected against the risk of DVT or PE. Failure to receive appropriate thromboprophylaxis can result in serious complications, including pulmonary embolism and death.

Bowel preparation: This is the process of cleansing the large bowel before a medical procedure or surgery. The goal of bowel preparation is to clear out any stool or debris from the colon, which can interfere with the accuracy of the medical procedure or surgery.

There are several methods for bowel preparation, and the specific method used may depend on the type of procedure or surgery being performed.

Some common methods include:

- Oral laxatives: These are medications that are taken by mouth to stimulate bowel movements and clear out the colon. Examples include polyethylene glycol (PEG) and magnesium citrate.
- Enemas: These involve the insertion of a solution into the rectum to stimulate bowel movements and clear out the lower part of the colon.
- Colonoscopy preparation: This involves a combination of oral laxatives and a clear liquid diet for a time before the procedure.

It is important to follow the instructions provided by your healthcare provider for bowel preparation to ensure that the colon is properly cleansed. Failure to adequately prepare the bowel can result in complications during the medical procedure or surgery.

A low residue diet: This is a type of diet that is often recommended before surgery or medical procedures that involve the digestive tract. The goal of this diet is to reduce the amount of residue or undigested food in the colon, which can make it difficult for healthcare providers to visualise the area during a medical procedure or surgery.

Foods that are typically limited when you are on a low residue diet include:

- High-fibre foods: These include fruits, vegetables, whole grains, nuts, and seeds.
- Dairy products: For some people, milk, cheese, and other dairy products can be difficult to digest .

➢ Meat and other proteins: red meats, fatty cuts of meat, and other high-protein foods can be difficult to digest and may increase the amount of residue in the colon.
➢ Spicy or fried foods: These can irritate the digestive tract and increase the risk of diarrhoea.

Foods that you are allowed on a low residue diet include:
➢ Refined grains: White bread, white rice, and other refined grains are generally easier to digest than whole grains.
➢ Lean proteins: Chicken, fish, eggs, and other lean proteins are generally easier to digest than red meats.
➢ Dairy substitutes: Lactose-free milk, soy milk, and other dairy substitutes may be allowed on a low residue diet.

It is important to follow the specific instructions given by your healthcare team for a low residue diet before surgery or medical procedures to ensure that the digestive tract is properly prepared. In some cases, a clear liquid diet may also be recommended in the day or two before the procedure.

> **Self Check-In: Bowel Prep Readiness**
>
> - **Do I understand what bowel preparation is required for my procedure?**
> - **Am I clear on how and when to take any laxatives?**
> - **If an enema is required, is this one I can do at home myself and do I know how to use it?**
> - **If or when I need to start a clear liquid or low residue diet, do I know what I can and can't eat?**
> - **How do I feel about the upcoming bowel prep process?**
> - **What planned activities or relaxation techniques can I use to stay calm and comfortable?**
> - **Am I clear on what to do and who to contact if I have any issues during the prep process**

Guide-wire insertion: An X-ray guide wire is a thin, flexible wire that is used to guide surgeons during breast surgery. The wire is typically inserted in the X-ray department on the day of surgery and is used to find and mark a suspicious or abnormal area of tissue that needs to be removed; its location is confirmed with the help of X-ray imaging.

The use of an X-ray guide wire can help to improve the accuracy of breast surgery and reduce the risk of complications. However, as with any medical procedure, there are potential risks and complications associated with the use of an X-ray guide wire, including bleeding, infection, and damage to surrounding tissue. Your healthcare provider will discuss the risks and benefits of this procedure with you before the surgery.

Enhanced recovery programmes

Depending on the nature of your procedure, you may be involved in an Enhanced Recovery Programme (ERP); these are sometimes known as Enhanced Recovery After Surgery (ERAS) Programmes too. This is a multidisciplinary approach to patient care that aims to improve the outcomes and experiences of patients undergoing surgery or other invasive procedures. The programme involves a set of evidence-based interventions and best practices that are designed to optimise patients' physical and emotional health before, during, and after surgery. Patients are educated about the ERP and what to expect before, during, and after surgery.

Studies have shown that an ERP can lead to significant improvements in patient outcomes, including reduced length of hospital stay, decreased rates of complications, and improved patient satisfaction.

The ERP focuses on reducing the stress and trauma associated with surgery, minimising pain and discomfort, and accelerating recovery. The specific elements of the programme will vary, depending on the type of surgery or procedure being performed, but they typically include the following components:

- *Pre-operative optimisation:* This involves a comprehensive assessment of the patient's physical and emotional health

before surgery, with a focus on optimising nutrition, hydration, and overall health.
- *Minimally invasive surgery:* Minimally invasive techniques, such as laparoscopic surgery or robotic surgery, are used whenever possible to reduce the trauma and stress of surgery.
- *Enhanced anaesthesia:* Advanced techniques, such as nerve blocks or regional anaesthesia, are used to minimise pain and reduce the need for opioids (strong painkillers such as morphine).
- *Early mobilisation:* Patients are encouraged to get out of bed and move around as soon as possible after surgery to reduce the risk of complications and accelerate recovery.
- *Early nutrition:* Patients are encouraged to start eating and drinking as soon as possible after surgery to promote healing and recovery.
- *Pain management:* A multimodal approach to pain management is often used, including non-opioid pain medications, nerve blocks, and other interventions.

Anaesthetic procedures you may need

Your anaesthetist is responsible for ensuring you are comfortable and pain-free during surgery. To achieve this goal, they may insert several different tubes and perform various procedures to help monitor and regulate your vital signs and administer medication. The specific lines and procedures used during surgery will vary depending on your medical condition, the type of surgery being performed, and the anaesthetists' preferences and experience. They will discuss these options with you before surgery and answer any questions you may have either at pre-operative assessment appointments or on the day of surgery.

Here are some of the lines and procedures that an anaesthetist may insert during surgery:

Common

- Intravenous (IV) cannula: This is a small tube that is inserted into a vein, usually in your arm or hand to supply access for medications, fluids, or blood transfusions.

- Endotracheal tube: This is a flexible tube that is inserted through your mouth or nose and down into the trachea to help you to breathe during surgery. These are not always needed, as other airway options are possible. The important thing for you to know is that usually this is done after you are under general anaesthesia, so you won't know it is happening. Very rarely will these need to be inserted while you are still awake, but your anaesthetist will clearly discuss this with you beforehand explaining why it is needed and what you should expect.

Uncommon

- Arterial line: This is a thin catheter that is inserted into an artery to monitor your blood pressure and blood gases. It is usually placed in your wrist, but other arteries can be used.
- Central venous catheter: This is a larger catheter that is inserted into a large vein in the neck, chest, or groin to check your fluid status and allow access for medications.
- Epidural catheter: This is a small tube that is inserted into your back near the spinal cord to supply pain relief during and after surgery.
- Nasogastric (NG) tube: This is a flexible tube that is inserted through your nose and down into your stomach to help decompress the stomach and prevent vomiting during surgery. This can be placed on the ward before you come to surgery or can be done while you are under general anaesthesia.

Post-operative care

Daycase surgery, also known as ambulatory surgery or outpatient surgery, refers to surgical procedures that are performed on an outpatient basis, where the patient is admitted to and discharged from the hospital or surgical facility on the same day. Daycase surgery is typically used for relatively minor surgical procedures that do not require an overnight hospital stay.

Examples of daycase surgeries include cataract surgery, hernia repair, diagnostic procedures like endoscopy and colonoscopy, and minor orthopaedic procedures such as arthroscopy. Daycase surgery also involves certain non-surgical procedures, such as chemotherapy or radiation therapy.

Daycase surgery offers several advantages, including shorter hospital stays, reduced healthcare costs, and a lower risk of hospital-acquired infections. However, not all patients are suitable for daycase surgery, and some may require overnight hospitalisation due to their medical condition or the complexity of the procedure.

Ward-based care refers to the medical care provided to patients in hospital wards, where they receive general medical care and attention from healthcare professionals, including doctors, nurses, and support staff. Ward-based care is typically provided to patients who are not critically ill or do not require the specialised medical interventions provided in the Intensive Care Units (ICU) or High Dependency Units (HDU).

The length of stay in a ward-based setting varies, depending on the patient's medical condition and the level of care needed. The goal of ward-based care is to promote the health and well-being of patients and help them recover from their surgery as quickly and safely as possible.

High dependency care is a level of medical care that is more intensive than general ward care but less intensive than ICU care. Patients in high dependency care require close monitoring and support but may not require the level of invasive monitoring or organ support provided in the ICU. They may require elevated levels of oxygen, frequent monitoring of vital signs, or intravenous medication or fluids.

Intensive care is a specialised form of medical care provided to patients who are critically ill or injured or have undergone major surgery or have significant pre-existing medical conditions. They require constant medical attention and support to keep their body systems functioning well. They may require mechanical ventilation, continuous kidney dialysis, medicines to support the heart, or other specialised interventions to support their vital signs. The intensive care unit is staffed by a team of highly trained medical professionals, including critical care doctors, nurses, respiratory therapists, and other specialists.

Allen's story

At the age of 68, Allen was scheduled for bowel surgery to treat his Crohn's disease. In the weeks leading up to the operation, he had several pre-op appointments and preparations.

First, Allen had a consultation with his surgeon to discuss the risks and benefits of the procedure and provide informed consent. His surgeon explained how she would perform the bowel resection laparoscopically to remove the damaged section of intestine.

Next, Allen had an appointment with the anaesthetist to go over the process before and during surgery. The doctor described how she would monitor Allen's vital signs and keep him comfortable.

Allen also had pre-op bloodwork, including testing his potassium and haemoglobin levels. Additionally, he underwent an ECG and chest X-ray to ensure his heart and lungs were healthy for surgery.

In the final weeks, a nurse practitioner reviewed Allen's medication list and had him stop blood-thinning and anti-inflammatory medications to minimise bleeding risks. Allen also adhered to a low-fibre diet and hydration guidelines to prepare his digestive system.

Thanks to this thorough prehab education, Allen knew exactly what to expect before his procedure. He felt informed, supported, and ready for his upcoming surgery.

Key takeaways

- ☐ Preparation for surgery is a complex process, but it is designed to achieve the best possible surgical outcome
- ☐ Talk to your medical team in order to fully understand your upcoming operation, and the purpose of any preparatory measures

Chapter 5

What to expect on the day of your procedure

"My job as a surgeon is ... to give my patients the encouragement and tools they need to speed up their recovery and leave my clinic better than they have been in years."

Kevin R. Stone

Nina was a bundle of nerves on the morning of her total hip replacement operation. The 54-year-old tried practising the deep breathing techniques she learned in prehab as nurses prepped her for surgery. But she was still feeling some anxiety....

The specific healthcare professionals you will see on the day of your surgery will vary, depending on the type of surgery and the policies of the healthcare facility. However, some common healthcare professionals you may meet include:

- Admissions nurses and healthcare assistants: These are the professionals who work in the admissions area you will report to on the day of surgery. This may be a specialised admissions unit or a ward. They will make sure you are prepared for surgery. A lot of surgical pathways involve standardised care, so expect to be asked a lot of questions as the nurses complete all the relevant admissions checklists and documents. It may seem as if a lot of information is needed, but it is all about making sure you are as safe as possible while in hospital. It is likely that you will be given a wristband to wear; has your identity information. It is worth noting that the location you are admitted to in the morning may not be the planned location of your post-operative care so it is worth asking this question on the day so you can tell your loved ones where to expect you to be after the procedure.

- Surgeon: The surgeon is the healthcare professional who will perform the surgery. They will come and see you on the day of surgery and check the consent form you have signed previously and answer any further questions you may have. If your surgery is happening on a specific side (e.g. left or right side) they may also draw on or mark your body with a marker pen to illustrate the location of the planned surgery. This forms part of a surgical safety checklist to ensure that the operation is performed on the correct side.
- Anaesthetist: This is the doctor who will assess your suitability for surgery that day and make sure you haven't had any changes to your health or medication since you were seen in the pre-assessment clinic. They are responsible for providing your anaesthesia and analgesia and will watch you closely during the surgery.
- Operating Department Practitioner or anaesthetic nurse: They will aid the surgeon and anaesthetist, and ensure they have all the drugs, equipment and monitoring that is needed.
- Theatre nurses: They will help the surgeon during the surgery and ensure that the surgical instruments and equipment are sterile.
- Surgical technicians: They will aid the surgeon during the surgery by handing them instruments and supplies.
- Recovery nurses: They will monitor your vital signs and help manage any pain or discomfort after the surgery.
- Physiotherapist: If your surgery requires rehabilitation, you may see a physical physiotherapist on the day of your surgery or during the following days.
- Specialist nurses: You may see a specialist nurse depending on your medical history, the procedure you are having, and the reasons for that procedure. This role is varied and may be different between hospitals but, as an example, it may be a nurse who specialises in enhanced recovery, cancer, stomas, or urinary catheters.
- Ward nurses and healthcare assistants: These professionals will look after you on the ward after your procedure and continue to care for you until you are ready for discharge from hospital. This would usually be back to your home but,

depending on your pre-procedure functional status, could be to a rehabilitation unit or nursing home.

It's important to note that this list is not comprehensive, and you may encounter additional healthcare professionals depending on your individual circumstances.

On the day of your surgery, you'll be asked to arrive at the hospital or clinic at a specific time. You may be asked to change into a hospital gown, to wear a wristband and to have your vital signs checked, such as your blood pressure, heart rate, and temperature.

A lot of hospitals have introduced the #callme initiative, which aims to improve the experience for patients who do not necessarily go by their birth name. It is a simple initiative where patients are given the opportunity to go by their preferred name.

This can include people who may wish to be addressed more formally as Mr or Mrs or people who use a middle name instead of their given birth name; people who use an abbreviated version of their name; or people who use a separate name, which is not necessarily a part of their formal identification data. Being in hospital can make people feel anxious or vulnerable but using the #callme system reassures patients and their friends and family that they will be addressed in the way that they choose.

It is likely that you will have been told to fast before arrival. Fasting before anaesthesia is an important safety measure to reduce the risk of aspiration, which is the accidental inhalation of stomach contents into the lungs. When a patient is under general anaesthesia, they can sometimes lose the ability to protect their airway reflexes, making it easier for stomach contents to enter the lungs.

It is usually recommended that patients should not eat solid foods for at least six hours before undergoing anaesthesia. Clear liquids, such as water, tea, black coffee, or fruit juices without pulp, can usually be consumed up to two hours before surgery and some areas use a 'sip until send' policy in which you are permitted to drink small amounts of water right up until you are transferred to the theatre complex.

However, it's important to check with your healthcare provider about their specific recommendations for fasting before your procedure, as individual circumstances and local policies may vary.

It's essential to follow the instructions provided by your healthcare provider regarding fasting before anaesthesia, as failure to do so can lead to serious complications during the procedure. If you have any concerns or questions about fasting before anaesthesia, be sure to discuss them with your healthcare team.

Due to the way surgical lists are planned, there may be other patients who are on the same list as you who are also asked to attend at the same time you are. The lists are usually separated into morning and afternoon lists but can be organised in other ways. While it may be frustrating, having to arrive early and then waiting around until it is your turn, it is the most efficient way to run the lists. The patients all need to be reviewed by the anaesthetist and surgeon on the day of surgery and it can be difficult to predict how long each operation will take, so it is not practical to give everyone a staggered arrival time. It is important to pack something to do while you are waiting, to keep yourself busy and distracted during the wait.

There can be other causes of delays in your scheduled surgery time. In some cases, unexpected events such as emergency surgeries or equipment malfunctions may cause delays in your scheduled surgery time. It's important to remember that delays can be frustrating, but they are often necessary to ensure a safe and successful surgery. If you have concerns about the wait time or any other aspect of your surgery, be sure to discuss them with your healthcare team.

When it is your turn, you will be taken to the operating theatre complex and then usually into an anaesthetic room where, once all the final checks and safety checklists are completed, you'll be given your anaesthetic and your surgery will be performed. Some institutions anaesthetise their patients in the theatre itself as they do not use anaesthetic rooms, but this is down to local procedures and policy.

The surgery itself may take several hours, depending on the complexity of the procedure. After the surgery is complete, you'll be taken to the recovery room, where you'll be closely monitored as the effects of the anaesthesia wear off. Once you are safe to be discharged from the recovery room you will be transferred to a post-operative ward or area.

Nina's story

While Nina was waiting, the anaesthetist stopped by to reassure her about the sedation process. Soon, it was time for her to be wheeled into the operating room. She took in the bright lights, surgical tools, and team of scrub-clad medical professionals awaiting her behind their masks.

Though nervous, Nina knew she was in the most capable hands. She felt relief seeing her orthopaedic surgeon, who she trusted completely after months of prehab preparation together. As the anaesthesia medications flowed into her IV, Nina recalled the calming nature photos from her visualisation practices. Within seconds, she was asleep.

In recovery, Nina awoke feeling groggy but remarkably little pain thanks to her epidural anaesthesia. The surgery was behind her, and she could now embark on healing. Nina was grateful for the prehab skills that had carried her smoothly through this intimidating surgical experience.

Waiting for a loved one who is undergoing surgery

If you have your surgery under general anaesthesia, you won't remember anything from the start of your anaesthetic to when you wake up in recovery. While you are undergoing your surgical procedure it can be hard for your family and friends as waiting for a loved one to come out of surgery can be a highly anxious and stressful experience. It's natural for them to feel worried and scared, as they may not know what's happening inside the operating room or how the surgery is going. During this time, they may feel a range of emotions, including fear, anticipation, and hope.

They might find themselves pacing or fidgeting, constantly checking their phone or watch, or staring off into space. They might even experience physical symptoms of stress, such as sweating, trembling, or difficulty breathing. It's important for them to take care of themselves during this time by trying to stay calm, taking deep breaths, and distracting themselves with something they enjoy or finding support from their friends or family.

The waiting period can be long, but it's crucial for them to stay patient. With your permission, the medical staff will keep them updated on your condition, and, once the surgery is over and you are in recovery or back on the ward, you should be able to contact them to let them know how it went. The surgeon may also contact your next of kin after the procedure to tell them how the procedure went. The important thing for your loved ones to remember is that no news is almost always good news. It always takes longer than you think for the surgery to be completed and the healthcare team to contact them but, if they haven't heard anything, they must not assume this is because something untoward has happened. It does just take time.

When a child is due to undergo a surgical procedure a parent or guardian will often go with them to the anaesthetic room and be present until their child is asleep.

The experience of watching your child undergo anaesthesia can be stressful and emotional for many parents and guardians. It is natural to feel anxious or worried about your child's safety and well-being during the procedure. However, it's important to remember that anaesthesia is a routine part of many medical procedures, and medical professionals are highly trained to ensure the safety and comfort of their patients. Remember that your child is well cared for, and the medical professionals are there to ensure their safety and well-being.

Key takeaways

- ☐ No matter how well prepared you are, the day of the surgery can be a strange experience
- ☐ Remember that you are in the hands of trained professionals, who have nothing but your best interests at heart
- ☐ Your prehabilitation process should help you to understand every aspect of the day of your operation

Chapter 6

What to expect after your procedure

"Opportunities to find deeper powers within ourselves come when life seems most challenging."

Joseph Campbell

After your surgery is completed and you have left the recovery room, you'll be moved to a hospital room or ward, where you'll be closely monitored by the healthcare team. You may have a drip or catheter in place, and you may need to stay in the hospital for a few days or longer depending on the type of surgery you had and your individual recovery.

After surgery, the types of symptoms or side-effects you might experience when waking up will depend on a range of factors, including the type of surgery, the anaesthesia used, your age, your overall health, and other individual factors. Here are some common symptoms and side effects that you might experience after surgery:

Pain or discomfort: Depending on the type of surgery, you may experience some pain or discomfort at the site of the incision or in other parts of your body. This is usually only mild but if you are in pain, you should let the recovery nurse know.

Nausea or vomiting: It's not uncommon to feel nauseous or vomit after surgery, especially if you have received general anaesthesia. The medical team can supply medication to help manage these symptoms.

Dizziness or confusion: You may feel groggy, disoriented, or confused when waking up from anaesthesia and surgery.

Sore throat or dry mouth: If you had a breathing tube inserted during surgery, you may have a sore throat afterwards. Certain medications that are used during your surgery can cause a dry mouth as a side effect. This symptom can be annoying, but it shouldn't last long.

Fatigue or weakness: Surgery and anaesthesia can be tiring on your body, and you may feel more tired than usual after waking up.

Temporary memory loss: Some people may experience temporary memory loss or difficulty remembering details immediately after waking up from anaesthesia.

It's important to remember that these symptoms and side effects are typically temporary, and should improve as you recover from surgery. Your medical team will watch you closely after surgery and supply any necessary medications or treatments to manage your symptoms and help you recover as quickly and safely as possible.

During your stay in the hospital, you'll be given pain medication to help manage any discomfort you may have. You'll also be encouraged to get up and move around as soon as possible to help prevent blood clots and other complications.

Before you're discharged from the hospital, you'll be given instructions on how to care for yourself at home, including any medications you need to take, any exercises you need to do, and any warning signs to watch out for. Make sure you know who to contact if you need advice after you get home.

After surgery, it's important to be aware of potential complications and to seek medical attention if you experience any concerning symptoms. Here are some common post-operative complications to watch for:

Infection: An infection can occur at the surgical site, leading to redness, swelling, warmth, pain, fever, or drainage.

Blood clots: Blood clots can form in the veins of the legs or pelvis, which can be dangerous if they break off and travel to the lungs. Symptoms of a blood clot include swelling, pain, redness, or warmth in the affected area.

Bleeding: Bleeding can occur at the surgical site or internally, leading to a drop in blood pressure, dizziness, or weakness.

Breathing problems: Breathing problems could occur after surgery, especially if you received general anaesthesia. Symptoms of this can include shortness of breath, chest pain, or coughing.

Pain or discomfort: Pain or discomfort can persist after surgery and may require more medication or treatment.

Other complications specific to the type of surgery: Depending on the type of surgery, there may be other potential complications to watch out for, such as bowel obstruction or urinary retention.

The type of recovery process you can expect will depend on a range of factors, including the type of surgery, the anaesthesia used, your age, your overall health, and other individual factors. However, here are some common aspects of the post-operative recovery process that you can generally expect:

Wound care: If you have a surgical incision, you will need to keep the area clean and dry to prevent infection. Your medical team will supply instructions on how to care for the wound and change any dressings. Surgical wounds, which may be covered by dressings and held by stitches, clips or glue. You'll get advice on how to care for these. If you have stitches or clips that need to be removed, you'll be advised where and when to have this done by your healthcare team.

Activity restrictions: After surgery, you may need to limit certain activities, such as heavy lifting or strenuous exercise, for some time to allow your body to heal.

Follow-up appointments: You will probably have follow-up appointments with your medical team to monitor your progress and ensure that your recovery is going smoothly.

Dietary changes: Depending on the type of surgery, you may need to amend your diet, such as avoiding certain foods or liquids.

Rehabilitation or physical therapy: If you had surgery on a joint or other body part, you may need to undergo rehabilitation or physical therapy to help you regain strength and range of motion.

Emotional support: Recovering from surgery can be emotionally challenging, and it's important to have a support system in place to help you through the process. Be kind to yourself; this can be a difficult and stressful period. If you find that your feelings of being down or upset don't go away over time, contact your GP.

> **SO HOW LONG WILL IT TAKE ME TO RECOVERY?**
>
> **The million-dollar question, and it may frustrate you when we say this ... but everyone is different. Your recovery depends on factors including the type of surgery, the anaesthesia used, your age, your overall health, and other individual factors.**

It's important to follow your doctor's instructions for post-operative care and attend any follow-up appointments as recommended. If you experience any symptoms that cause concern, or you have questions about your recovery, don't hesitate to reach out to your medical team for guidance.

Ray's story

At the age of 72, Ray underwent triple bypass heart surgery. As part of his prehab program, he had learned recovery would be difficult. However, the reality proved even more challenging than expected.

The early days brought discomfort, difficulty moving, sleeping problems, and relying on others for basic needs. Ray's mood plummeted as his independence was stripped away. He felt hopeless thinking about the long road ahead.

Thankfully, Ray had the support of his loving wife, Jenny. She sat with Ray during long, painful days in the hospital. At home, she took over chores Ray couldn't manage, like lifting objects or driving. Jenny also set small daily goals like making the bed or getting dressed to motivate Ray.

Ray's cardiologist and physical therapist gave him the tools and encouragement to rebuild his strength through walking and exercise. He celebrated each new milestone, no matter how small.

Looking back now, Ray realises his recovery was not linear – some days got better fast while others felt like setbacks. However, focusing on progress and support from Jenny kept Ray's spirits up. Six months later, Ray is doing regular cardio exercise and feels stronger than before his surgery. He is filled with gratitude for this second chance at life.

Helping yourself recover well

The best way to help yourself recover after surgery is to follow all the advice your doctors, nurses and other healthcare professionals give you. This advice will be specific to you, considering your circumstances and the treatment you had.

How long it takes you to recover and return to your normal activities after your operation depends on a variety of things, including your general health and the treatment you had. As we said, everyone is different. Your doctor will be able to give you an idea of how long it might take for you to return to your normal daily activities and exercise. They will give you advice about any restrictions on your activities after your surgery. In general, it's good to build up any activity gradually. Ask your doctor about specific leisure activities or sports that you want to resume or start.

Things you can do to help you recover more quickly include:

- Eat healthily. A healthy diet will supply all the nutrients your body needs to heal itself.
- Stop smoking. If you did not manage to quit before your surgery, make the decision not to smoke again. If you feel that isn't possible, at least try not to smoke during your recovery

period, or significantly reduce the number of cigarettes each day. Reach out for support on giving up – we know how hard it is and there are a lot of resources to help you make this giant leap to help your recovery.
- Get into a routine. Waking up at the same time each day and starting with a morning routine that gets you up and dressed and ready to start your day can be a benefit. Your recovery will not be linear, and you can expect good and bad days so rest when you need to but try to stick to a daily routine to help you get back to your normal day-to-day life.
- Accept help and support from family and friends. Now is the time to ask for help from your loved ones. They will be able to help with certain things that you might find difficult during this recovery period, such as shopping, heavy lifting or driving. Having support from loved ones, even if it is just a chat over coffee – can help keep your spirits up and a positive mood.

You may find it helpful to keep a journal of your recovery and progress, setting yourself achievable daily goals to encourage yourself. Depending on what surgery you have had, you should be ready for it to take you weeks or even months to feel fully recovered and back to normal. Your body will need time to heal properly, and this is often underestimated by patients.

Driving after an operation

If you have had a general anaesthesia or sedation, you should not drive for at least 24 hours after the procedure, as the effects of the medication may still be present in your system.

It is also important to note that driving while under the influence of medication can be dangerous, as some medications can cause drowsiness or impair your reaction time. Be sure to check with your doctor about any medication you are taking, and whether it is safe to drive.

If you feel unsure or uncomfortable about driving after your operation, it is always best to ask for help from a friend or family member or consider alternative transportation options such as a taxi or public transportation. Your safety is the top priority, and it is better to err on the side of caution when it comes to driving after an operation.

Resuming specialist activities after an operation

After undergoing general anaesthesia and surgery, it is important to avoid any hazardous activities that could pose a risk to your health or slow down your recovery process. It is important to follow your doctor's instructions, and to avoid any activities that could jeopardise your health or hinder your recovery process

Some examples of hazardous activities to avoid include:

- Operating heavy machinery. This requires focus, attention, and coordination, which may be impaired after surgery.
- Drinking alcohol can interact with anaesthesia and pain medications, leading to adverse effects such as drowsiness, dizziness, and impaired judgement.
- Strenuous physical activity can increase the risk of bleeding, pain, and other complications after surgery. It is important to avoid lifting heavy objects, taking part in contact sports, or engaging in other physically demanding activities until you have fully recovered.
- Air travel can be safe, but it depends on the type of surgery and how long it has been since the operation. In general, most people can fly after minor surgeries, such as dental procedures or biopsies, within a few days to a week after the operation. However, for major surgeries, such as abdominal surgery or joint replacement surgery, it is generally recommended to wait at least two to four weeks before flying. Flying after surgery could increase the risk of complications such as blood clots, especially if the surgery involved the legs or abdomen. This is because sitting for prolonged periods of time in a cramped aeroplane seat can reduce blood flow to the legs, increasing the risk of blood clots. If you have had surgery, your doctor may recommend that you wear compression stockings or take blood thinners to reduce this risk.

In addition, flying can also cause discomfort or pain if you have had surgery, especially if you need to sit in a particular position for a long time. It's important to discuss any concerns you have about flying with your doctor, who can advise you on when it is safe to fly and what precautions you should take. Your doctor may also recommend that you avoid air travel altogether until you have fully recovered from your surgery.

Diving is not generally recommended after an operation, especially if the surgery involved general anaesthesia or major abdominal or chest surgery. Diving involves exposure to high pressure, which can affect the body's ability to heal and may cause complications such as pain, bleeding, or damage to surgical incisions. It is important to consult with your doctor before considering diving after an operation. Your doctor can evaluate your individual case and advise you on when it may be safe to resume diving activities. In general, it is recommended to wait at least four to six weeks after surgery before diving. This allows the body to heal properly and reduces the risk of complications.It is also important to watch out for any signs of pain, discomfort, or unusual symptoms during and after diving, and to seek medical attention if any issues arise.

Key takeaways

- ☐ Bear in mind that surgery is stressful on your body, so you need to be careful about certain activities afterwards
- ☐ Listen to the advice of your medical team, as it will help you to recover as safely as possible

Summary and conclusions

Appendix 1

Glossary of terms

A

Anaesthesia: The administration of medications to induce a temporary loss of sensation or consciousness, ensuring pain-free surgery and a comfortable experience.

Anaesthetist: A medical doctor who specialises in administering anaesthesia and monitoring patients' vital signs during surgery.

Aseptic technique: Practices to prevent the introduction of infectious agents during surgery, maintaining a sterile environment.

B

Biopsy: Removal of a small tissue sample for diagnostic examination.

C

Catheter: Flexible tube inserted into the body to remove or introduce fluids.

Complications: Unforeseen medical issues that can arise during or after surgery, requiring additional treatment or management.

Consent form: A legal document that patients sign to indicate their understanding of the surgical procedure and its risks. This constitutes their agreement to undergo the surgery.

D

Daycase Surgery: Surgery that allows the patient to go home on the same day as the procedure, if there are no complications.

E

Elective Surgery: Non-emergency surgical procedure chosen by the patient and surgeon to improve health or quality of life.

Endoscope: Device with a camera used to observe internal organs and structures during minimally invasive surgery.

G

General anaesthesia: A state of unconsciousness induced by medications, allowing the patient to undergo surgery without feeling pain or discomfort.

H

Haemostasis: Process of controlling bleeding during surgery.

Haemorrhage: Excessive bleeding that can occur during or after surgery, which may require additional interventions.

I

Incision: A surgical cut made on the body to access the area requiring treatment or surgery.

Infection: Introduction of harmful microorganisms into the body, leading to inflammation and illness.

Informed Consent: Ethical and legal process through which patients receive detailed information about a procedure's risks, benefits, and alternatives before giving their permission to proceed with surgery.

Inpatient Surgery: Surgery that requires the patient to stay in the hospital overnight or for an extended period to recover and receive specialised care.

L

Laparoscopy: Minimally invasive surgical technique that uses small incisions and a camera-equipped scope.

Local anaesthesia: The numbing of a specific area of the body using medications, allowing for a procedure to be performed without feeling pain in that area.

M

Minimally Invasive Surgery: Techniques that involve smaller incisions, reducing trauma and recovery time.

N

Necrosis: Death of tissue, caused by inadequate blood supply.

O

Operating Theatre: Sterile environment where surgical procedures take place.

P

Perioperative: Referring to the entire surgical process, including pre-operative, intraoperative, and post-operative stages.

Post-operative Care: The medical attention and monitoring provided to patients after surgery to ensure a safe and successful recovery.

Prehabilitation: also known as prehab, refers to a program of exercise, nutrition, and other interventions that are designed to prepare a patient for an upcoming medical procedure, such as surgery or cancer treatment.

Pre-operative Assessment: The evaluation of a patient's health status and medical history before surgery to ensure they are well-prepared for the procedure.

Prognosis: Predicted outcome and course of a medical condition.

R

Recovery area: A specialised area where patients are closely monitored as they wake up from anaesthesia after surgery.

Rehabilitation: The process of recovering and regaining function after surgery, often involving physical therapy or other treatments.

Resection: Surgical removal of part or all an organ.

S

Scarring: The formation of a visible mark on the skin at the site of an incision after surgery.

Sterilisation: The process of eliminating all microorganisms and their spores from surgical instruments and equipment.

Subcutaneous: Beneath the skin.

Surgeon: A medical doctor who specialises in performing surgical procedures to treat various medical conditions.

Suture or stitch: Thread used to stitch incisions and wounds.

T

Theatre: A sterile environment where surgical procedures are performed, equipped with specialised medical equipment and instruments.

Tourniquet: Device used to temporarily stop blood flow to a limb during surgery.

Tumour: Abnormal growth of tissue, which can be cancerous (malignant) or non-cancerous (benign).

U

Ultrasound: Imaging technique using sound waves to visualise internal structures.

V

Venipuncture: Puncture of a vein for blood sampling or cannula placement.

W

Wound Dehiscence: Separation or splitting open of a surgical wound.

Appendix 2

Considerations specific for prehabilitation for different types of surgery

It's important to note that the specifics of prehabilitation will depend on the patient's individual health status, the type of surgery, and the recommendations of the medical team. Prehabilitation programs are typically customised for each patient to ensure the best possible outcomes. Patients should always consult with their healthcare providers before initiating any prehabilitation program, as well as following their medical team's guidance closely.

The specific implications of prehabilitation can vary depending on the type of surgery.

Orthopaedic Surgery (e.g., joint replacement, spine surgery):

- Prehabilitation may involve exercises to improve muscle strength, joint flexibility, and overall mobility in the affected area.
- Cardiovascular fitness may be addressed to improve circulation and stamina, as these surgeries can be physically demanding.
- Focus on maintaining or improving bone density and balance to prevent falls and fractures.
- Flexibility and balance exercises to reduce the risk of falls during recovery.
- Education on post-surgery exercises and mobility techniques.

Cardiac Surgery (e.g., heart bypass, valve replacement):

- Cardiovascular conditioning is crucial, including aerobic exercises to improve heart and lung function.

- Blood pressure and cholesterol management through lifestyle changes (for instance, to diet and exercise) can contribute to better cardiovascular health.
- Breathing exercises and lung capacity improvement are important to aid recovery after surgery.
- Stress management techniques to reduce anxiety and promote relaxation.
- Smoking cessation if applicable, as smoking can hinder healing.

Cancer Surgery (e.g., tumour removal):
- Maintaining or improving overall physical fitness can help the body tolerate the stress of surgery and enhance recovery.
- Nutritional assessment and interventions to ensure adequate nutrient intake and maintain muscle mass.
- Psychological support to manage stress and anxiety related to the cancer diagnosis.
- Coordination with oncology teams to ensure safe exercise considering cancer treatment effects.

Abdominal Surgery (e.g., hernia repair, gallbladder removal):
- Core strength and stability exercises to support the abdominal region and aid in post-operative mobility.
- Breathing exercises to promote lung expansion and prevent respiratory complications.
- Nutrition optimisation to support wound healing, tissue repair, and prevent constipation
- Bowel health management through dietary adjustments and hydration.

Pulmonary Surgery (e.g., lung resection):
- Respiratory exercises to enhance lung capacity and function, helping to prevent post-operative respiratory complications.
- Smoking cessation if applicable, to improve lung health and reduce risks associated with surgery.

Bariatric Surgery (e.g., weight loss surgery):

- Weight loss and lifestyle modifications before surgery can lead to safer and more effective outcomes.
- Nutritional counselling to prepare for dietary changes post-surgery.
- Physical activity and muscle-building exercises to maintain lean body mass and improve metabolism.
- Psychological counselling to address the emotional and behavioural aspects of eating.

Neurosurgery (e.g., brain or spinal surgery):

- Exercises to maintain or improve muscular strength and coordination, especially if surgery affects mobility. Core strengthening exercises to support the spine. Flexibility exercises to maintain spinal mobility.
- Mental exercises, mindfulness, and relaxation techniques to manage stress and anxiety.
- Education and support for the patient and their caregivers to prepare for potential changes in cognitive and physical function.

Appendix 3

Summary chart of different types of prehabilitation and lifestyle medicine approaches, interventions, and potential goals

Category	Approaches/ Interventions	Potential Goals
Physical Activity	- Aerobic exercises	- Improve cardiovascular health
	- Strength training	- Increase muscle mass and strength
	- Flexibility and mobility exercises	- Enhance range of motion and flexibility
	- Balance exercises	- Reduce risk of falls
Nutrition	- Balanced diet	- Maintain healthy weight
	- Portion control	- Support metabolic health
	- Adequate hydration	- Improve digestion
	- Nutrient-dense foods	- Enhance overall energy levels
Stress Management	- Mindfulness meditation	- Reduce stress and anxiety

Category	Approaches/Interventions	Potential Goals
	- Deep breathing techniques	- Improve emotional well-being
	- Progressive muscle relaxation	- Enhance sleep quality
	- Yoga or tai chi	- Promote relaxation
Sleep Hygiene	- Consistent sleep schedule	- Optimise cognitive function
	- Dark and quiet sleep environment	- Support immune system
	- Limiting screen time before bed	- Enhance mood and mental clarity
	- Avoiding heavy meals close to bedtime	- Prevent sleep disturbances
Smoking and Alcohol	- Smoking cessation programs	- Reduce risk of chronic diseases
	- Moderation in alcohol consumption	- Improve liver and cardiovascular health
Screen Time	- Setting screen time limits	- Enhance focus and productivity
	- Taking breaks from screens	- Improve posture
Social Connections	- Maintaining relationships	- Enhance emotional support
	- Participating in social activities	- Reduce feelings of isolation
Hygiene Practices	- Regular handwashing	- Prevent illness transmission
	- Dental hygiene	- Maintain oral health
	- Proper sanitation practices	- Minimise risk of infections

Category	Approaches/ Interventions	Potential Goals
Mind-Body Practices	- Biofeedback	- Improve mind-body connection
	- Visualisation techniques	- Enhance mental resilience
	- Cognitive-behavioural therapy	- Address negative thought patterns

Appendix 4

Resources and support for patients

In the UK, patients undergoing surgery have access to a variety of resources to help them prepare for and recover from their procedures. Some of the key resources available include:

The National Health Service (NHS): The NHS provides comprehensive information about surgical procedures, pre-operative and post-operative care, and what to expect during recovery. The NHS website has a dedicated section on surgery that offers guidance and resources specific to various surgical procedures.

Surgical clinics and hospitals: Your healthcare provider or surgeon's office will provide you with information about your specific surgery, including pre-operative instructions, what to expect during the procedure, and post-operative care guidelines. They can answer any questions you have about your surgery.

Patient information leaflets: Many hospitals and clinics provide patient information leaflets that explain the surgical procedure, potential risks, benefits, and post-operative care instructions. These leaflets are often given to patients during their pre-operative appointments.

Pre-operative assessment appointments: Before surgery, you may be asked to attend a pre-operative assessment clinic. This is where healthcare professionals will assess your overall health, perform necessary tests, and provide you with information on how to prepare for surgery, including fasting instructions and medication management.

Surgical consent: Your surgeon will discuss the details of your surgery, including the potential risks and benefits. They will ask for your informed consent before proceeding with the procedure. Make sure to ask any questions you have and that you fully understand the procedure before signing the consent form.

Anaesthesia information: If you'll be receiving anaesthesia, you'll receive information about the type of anaesthesia you'll be given and what to expect during and after the procedure. Anaesthesia teams are available to answer your questions and address any concerns.

Rehabilitation and recovery resources: Depending on the type of surgery, you might be referred to physical therapy, occupational therapy, or other rehabilitation services to help you recover and regain your strength and mobility after surgery.

Pain management: Information about pain management strategies and medications you may be prescribed post-surgery will be provided to you. Make sure to follow your healthcare provider's instructions for pain relief.

Online resources: The NHS website and other reputable healthcare websites may have information on specific surgical procedures, recovery tips, and resources for patients undergoing surgery.

Support groups: Some hospitals or healthcare organisations offer support groups for patients undergoing surgery. These groups can provide emotional support, share experiences, and offer advice for a smoother recovery.

Remember that every surgery is unique, so the resources available to you may vary depending on the type of surgery you're having and the hospital or clinic you're receiving care from. It's important to communicate openly with your healthcare team and ask any questions you must ensure you're well-informed and prepared for your surgery.

Acknowledgements

First and foremost, we would like to express our deepest appreciation to our families:

Sunil's wife Naina and his daughters Advika and Avishka as well as his parents, have all provided him with unfaltering support during the writing and editing process.

Toni's husband James has offered valuable insights, encouragement, and constructive feedback throughout and Bobby and Ella played a role in shaping and refining this work.

We will both be forever grateful for their guidance and dedication to supporting us in this book.

Secondly, we are humbled and honoured to have been successfully elected to serve as Council Members of the Royal College of Anaesthetists together. We are grateful that despite completing our Lifestyle Medicine qualifications at the same time, our paths were yet to cross until the moment we joined Council together and realised our shared passion in this field and began this friendship. We would like to extend our heartfelt gratitude to our colleagues on Council who have provided tremendous support and inspiration. Their stimulating discussion and insightful suggestions have greatly enriched our understanding and perspective on the need for this book.

Last but certainly not least, we wish to convey our heartfelt appreciation to the experts and professionals who generously dedicated their time and shared their insights, to help us shape this book. Their invaluable contributions have undeniably elevated the overall quality of this work.

In particular, our deepest gratitude goes to Tony Wrighton, whose unwavering support, guidance, and encouragement have been instrumental in transforming this project into the tangible form of this book. His belief in our vision has propelled us forward and has been an inspiration to us during this process.

Printed in Great Britain
by Amazon